Hurt on the Job:

A Guide to the Massachusetts Workers Compensation System

Second Edition

Printed by the Massachusetts Nurses Association: Canton, MA.

ISBN 13: 978-0-615-15386-5

Acknowledgments:

Principal Author: Nancy Ann Foley

Contributing Authors: Katherine Smith, Esq.
Philip S. Korman
Richard Fontaine, Esq.
Francesca Rheannon
Cynthia Tarail

Research Assistant: Julie Roda

Contributing Reviewers:

Mike Florio, Esq.   John Thoma
Aaron Wilson   Nancy Lessin
Patricia Walsh   Doreen McDonald
Alice Briere   Penny Ford
Robert Quinn, Esq.   Veronica Levesque
Craig Robinson, Esq.   Marcy Goldstein-Gelb
Robert Schwartz, Esq.   Charles Casartello, Esq.
David Engle, Esq.   Carla Dell'Olio
Pamela Manson, Esq.   Jon Weissman
Katherine Smith, Esq.   Paul Bradford Brousseau, Esq.

Special acknowledgment in loving memory of Aaron D. Wilson, executive director of Western MassCOSH from 2001-2006. Mr. Wilson worked tirelessly to see this book published, but died suddenly before its publication.

About Western MassCOSH

The Western Massachusetts Coalition for Occupational Safety and Health has been in existence since 1976, first as a branch office of the Boston-based MassCOSH, then as an independent organization since 1991. MassCOSH was founded by a coalition of labor and community organizations together with activist unionists, injured workers and professionals. Their common goal was to combat workplace injuries and illnesses. Western MassCOSH membership consists of union locals, workers, injured workers and legal professionals. The goal of Western MassCOSH is to help create safer and healthier work environments. These goals are accomplished through training and education programs, heath and legal assistance (including referral), advocacy and political action.

Over the years, Western MassCOSH has responded to thousands of requests for assistance from workers on health and safety problems. We have co-sponsored conferences on the Right to Know Law, OSHA, Hispanic Workers Health and Safety, Toxic Use Reduction, and Organizing for Diversity. Western MassCOSH has been instrumental in the passage of state laws on right to know, asbestos, lead paint and whistle-blowing protection.

Since 1996, Western MassCOSH has been supporting and sponsoring the Alliance for Injured Workers (originally called Injured Workers' Resources). The Alliance holds monthly support group meetings, often featuring speakers of interest to injured workers. It publishes the *Injured Workers Survival Guide*, a directory of services in Hampden and Hampshire counties. The alliance has an advisory board made up primarily of injured workers. Members of the alliance often accompany each other to court hearings and medical appointments. They also work to change laws by giving testimony at legislative hearings and by talking to legislators.

640 Page Boulevard, Springfield, MA 01104, 413-731-0760
www.afiw.org (Alliance for Injured Workers website)

PREFACE

I learned about the workers compensation system the hard way - by filing a claim in the mid-1990s. I found the Western Massachusetts Coalition for Occupational Safety and Health through a small notice in the newspaper advertising a meeting of the coalition's support group for injured workers. The group was then called Injured Workers' Resources, but we have since changed our name to the Alliance for Injured Workers.

While fighting the system, I felt confused, angry, frightened and even desperate. The injured workers group was a lifeline. Eventually, I became director of the alliance, and a couple of years ago I set out to rewrite *Hurt on the Job: A Guide to the Massachusetts Workers Compensation System*, a book first published by Western MassCOSH in 1995. The principal author of the 1995 edition was Philip S. Korman, Western MassCOSH executive director at that time.

I interviewed injured workers and included their experiences (as well as a few of my own) in this book. Quotes from injured workers are sprinkled throughout the chapters. This second edition is not simply a guide to what the law says is supposed to happen. It is about what really *does* happen to thousands of injured workers each year. We also have a new section on federal workers compensation written by Katherine Smith, Esq., an attorney from Palmer, Mass.

Writing this book presented a physical challenge, since I have repetitive strain injury and trouble sitting for very long. I'm grateful to the Massachusetts Rehabilitation Commission for providing me with a new computer and Dragon speech program to replace my old equipment that was not up to the task. Large portions of this book were written while I was lying down, talking to the computer.

We are thrilled to offer this book because it is an opportunity to give injured workers the information we wish we had known when we were first injured. It is a warning to help injured workers avoid the mistakes that we made.

Nancy Ann Foley
Senior Program Director
Western MassCOSH

TABLE OF CONTENTS

SECTION I: THE MASSACHUSETTS SYSTEM

SECTION II: FEDERAL WORKERS COMPENSATION

SECTION I

THE MASSACHUSETTS SYSTEM

The comp system is not there to pay you. It took me 10 years to learn that. They shouldn't even call it the comp system. That gives you the understanding that someone is there to help you. They're really not. It's an antagonistic system to make money. I didn't learn that until it was too late.

◆

My impression is that up to a certain extent, it's helpful for some people, but beyond a certain point it's unhelpful to most everyone. If you have a condition which improves within a short amount of time, and you've been able to benefit from wage replacement while ill, it works as well as can be expected. It seems that if you have a problem that goes on for a long time, or longer than the insurance company thinks it should, then it becomes a tug-of-war.

◆

I think the whole system is a sham.

INTRODUCTION

The popular image of injured workers has little to do with reality. Television news programs occasionally show film of an injured worker performing heavy labor or playing sports. Co-workers may think injured colleagues are enjoying a "vacation." For many people, however, fighting for workers comp benefits is a nightmare. The physical pain and limitations from the injury are only the beginning. Just as painful is trying to make sense of an unfair system. Employees who worked hard for years do not understand why the insurer is fighting their claim. They become desperate when they have no income for weeks or months. They may fall into serious financial difficulty, losing their homes and savings.

The law is not on our side. A "reform" in 1991 of the Massachusetts workers compensation system was a major setback for injured workers. Supported by employers, business groups and their insurance allies, the "reform" (Massachusetts General Laws, Chapter 152) cut benefits and hurt injured workers in other ways. We explain how this law works, what is wrong with it, how we might change it, and how to survive under it while it remains the law.

This 1991 Massachusetts law does *not* apply to federal workers, police and firefighters or certain municipal employees, as well as workers injured before Dec. 23, 1991. We have a separate section of this book that explains the federal workers comp system. Of course, we cannot explain every aspect of the law, so use this book as a guide, not as a substitute for professional legal advice.

CHAPTER 1

HOPE FOR THE BEST; PREPARE FOR THE WORST

I didn't think anything bad could happen. Boy, was I wrong.

She was the victim of violence in the workplace. Her injuries left her in constant pain. She continued to try to work, but missed so many days that her employer finally told her she would have to leave.

> *After literally more than five years of trying alternative ways to keep working, things were really bad. I went to a meeting [with the employer]. They were there to tell me I wasn't coming back. I literally broke down. I couldn't hold it together. That was the end. It just wasn't working. By the summer of 1997, I wasn't going back. That's a long time to try daily, weekly, every other day. Like so many of us, I didn't want to believe. I just kept expecting that I was going to be better.*

For nearly seven years after the injury, she saw no reason to get a lawyer. "Those first seven years, I talked with the adjustor regularly. When people told me to get a lawyer, I thought, 'Why? They are doing everything for me.'" She did not understand the time limits on certain benefits or that she would have to file (and fight for) permanent and total disability benefits. "I just thought, 'I'm hurt, so I get workers comp, and I'm not getting better, so I keep getting it.'"

Eventually, she hired a lawyer and applied for permanent, total disability. The fight turned nasty. The insurer began sending private investigators to follow her. The first time was, ironically, the day she attended a meeting of the Alliance for Injured Workers where the topic was surveillance! As she listened to the speaker, she thought, "Well, that's for other people. They don't need to follow me. There were witnesses; they know I'm hurt." She found out later that she had been followed to that meeting and filmed by a private investigator! Meanwhile, she was being treated at pain clinics and given strong medication so that she could have some quality of life.

> *With all the medicine I take, I'm still never without pain, never ever, since 1992... Each day has to be situated with a lot of down time to have some times up. Some days that doesn't work. Some days it's pain from beginning to end. Because it's my spine, it affects everything else. It's agony that no amount of medication takes away.*

She became depressed and asked the workers comp insurer to pay for treatment, not realizing that this would open the door for the insurer to get copies of the treatment notes and demand records from all her previous mental health providers. She was offered a settlement prior to the hearing, but turned it down. "I thought everything about my story makes them look like they are doing the wrong thing. I felt I had a win-win case." She did not know that the lawyer for the insurer would come to the hearing armed with her mental health records. "I didn't know how bad it would be. I didn't really know they were going to have my psych records. Prior to that I thought, what could they ask me? I didn't think anything bad could happen. Boy, was I wrong. Just the fact that they could read all that stuff."

The lawyer harped on a reference to her helping her sister move. This was an error in the therapist's notes. This injured worker had babysat her sister's children, while her sister packed. She was able to explain this as well as other points the lawyer tried to raise, and the information in the records did not prove damaging. Nevertheless, being grilled in this fashion was traumatic. "That was God awful. It was an hour and a half [on the stand], and I cried the whole time."

After the hearing, the decision came in the mail. The judge had approved total and permanent disability benefits. "When I read it and re-read it, it felt like someone other than my family was understanding how much I had gone through and how hard I tried to support myself and keep working. For that short term, I felt like my troubles were over, and I was on easy street. I think naive would be a good word."

She soon discovered that her troubles were not over. Three months after the judgment, the insurer sent her to one of its own doctors, ironically called an "independent" medical examiner. "And three months later, they sent me to another one. That is when I realized that it was never ending." Private investigators continued to follow her. "I thought that was all over when I got my judgment. It was pretty shocking to realize nothing had changed."

She lived like this for many years. She also had trouble getting reimbursement for the expensive pain medication she needs. The insurer tried again to use her therapy records against her. The records were given to another independent medical examiner who, before meeting her, wrote a 15-page report, called a "records review." He interpreted comments she had made to therapists years before her injury as evidence that she did not want to work.

He had taken the psych records and woven in pieces and parts that went back in the record until when I was first in college, years before my injury. He wove all of those self-doubt processes that you talk about with a psychiatrist or psychologist into a profile of a drug-dependent, possibly alcoholic person who didn't want to work a day in her life. I hadn't seen him yet...Here I was someone who tried for years and years to work only to read that I had always had a problem with being devoted to hard work. It was a profile of somebody who was not me. He was getting paid to make me look bad.

This injured worker finally accepted a settlement that was less than two years salary. "I felt it was a slap in the face. How anyone thinks they could live on that for the rest of their life, it was absolutely beyond belief." She felt fortunate to have a supportive family. "The final settlement was shockingly low! Knowing that I had the support of family and other resources has kept me moving forward. It's hard to think there were people who got that tiny settlement and that was it." Her injury and the adversarial system have not been the only sources of her pain.

I've heard comments like:

"Well, you don't look hurt, you look so healthy."

"What do I have to do to get all that time off?"

"Must be nice having a nice car when you're not working."

"How do I get that money?"

"Well, you don't look bad."

"What do you know about job hunting? You haven't worked in 10 years."

Will this happen to you?

Not every case will become as adversarial as this one. Some cases run smoothly from start to finish. Sometimes the insurer immediately takes an adversarial stance. Some injured workers are treated well initially, but hassled as the case drags on and becomes more costly. It became clear to us while researching this book that almost every injured worker whose case was difficult began the process thinking that it would run smoothly. They had legitimate injuries and expected to be treated fairly. They were taken by surprise when the insurer contested their case. Even the extent of their disability was not clear at first. Several injured workers with chronic conditions explain how they initially expected to recover and return to work. It was often only after years of failed work attempts and failed medical treatments that they realized they would never be part of the work force again.

What can you learn from the experience of others?

This book includes many anecdotes from injured workers whose experience with the system was as painful as or more painful than their injuries. The point is not to scare you, but to prepare you. Let's consider the injured worker described above. She did not hire a lawyer for many years. We explain the importance of seeking legal help in the early stages. She did not understand the time limits for various types of benefits. These are explained in Chapter 5. This injured worker had every right to try to make the insurer pay for therapy. Nevertheless, such a claim must be made with full understanding of the possible consequences. This is discussed in Chapter 4. Several chapters in this book discuss the role independent medical examiners play in the process.

This case demonstrates that even when an injured worker "wins" in court, he or she can go through tremendous emotional stress and harassment. There is no jackpot awaiting injured workers who win their cases. Early chapters give some basic information about filing a claim and collecting benefits. Later chapters deal with contested claims and issues that pertain to living with a long-term disability. We suggest you read all of the chapters, even if you have not yet had any problems. Hope for the best, but prepare for the worst.

CHAPTER 2

IS IT A WORKERS COMP CASE?

I went home thinking maybe it would just require rest over the weekend. When I woke up the next morning on Sunday, I could not move my neck. It felt like bone on bone and in fact, it was. That was my last time to ever work…I wasn't facing reality that I wasn't going back.

You have been injured at work. What should you do now? Perhaps the injury happened in front of everyone, you were rushed to the emergency room, and your employer has already reported your injury. Perhaps you feel pain a day or two after lifting heavy boxes, but you are hesitant to tell your employer. You tell yourself that maybe the pain will go away. Or, perhaps your hands and arms have been hurting for months as a result of typing, but you have not reported your injury or even seen a doctor. You know you have an injury or an illness. Do you have a workers comp case? In this chapter, we explain the criteria you need to consider to answer this question. We also explain the difference between occupational injuries and occupational illnesses.

Where did the injury happen?

If you are hurt on company property, your injury is usually covered. Injuries that occur while you are making deliveries or special trips related to work, driving to a work-related training, or traveling from your home to a work site off your employer's premises (e.g., home health aide), are probably covered, also. Injuries that probably would *not* be covered include those that occur off the premises, during lunch or break, on the way to work or on the way home, or work-sponsored activities that you choose to attend, such as a company picnic or softball game. The Massachusetts General Laws state that personal injury "shall not include any injury resulting from an employee's purely voluntary participation in any recreational activity, including but not limited to athletic events, parties, and picnics, even though the employer pays some or all of the costs thereof" (M.G.L. Ch. 152, Sec. 1). If you work for a Massachusetts employer and are hurt in another state, you may be able to collect under the other state's system. Discuss this with a lawyer.

What if an employer has no workers comp insurance?

Employers are required to have workers comp insurance. They can buy it from an insurance company or apply to the Department of Industrial Accidents (DIA) to be self-insured. The DIA can issue a stop-work order that would prevent an uninsured employer from doing business, and it can fine the employer $100 per day until insurance is obtained. The DIA's Workers Compensation Trust Fund pays benefits to employees of an uninsured employer. The employer may also be sued for lost wages, medical bills, pain and suffering, and other damages. Call 877-MASSAFE, ext. 214, to report an uninsured employer.

Can you be compensated for a disease or illness?

Determining whether or not you have a claim is easy with many injuries, such as falling off a platform, getting fingers caught in machinery, or lifting heavy boxes and hurting your back. You can easily describe the cause of the injury and when and where it happened. The comp system was designed to compensate workers for these types of obvious injuries.

There is another category of cases that involve occupational illnesses and diseases. These include repetitive strain injuries, lung disease, and chemical injuries. These cases are generally harder to prove and harder to win than accident cases, especially if your condition develops years later. You are more likely to receive workers comp if you contract a disease recognized as a hazard of your occupation. If you are a hospital worker, for example, you will probably be covered if you contract hepatitis B from a patient.

What if a pre-existing condition is made worse by a work injury?

If your job worsens a pre-existing condition, you may still receive benefits if what occurred on the job remains a "major, but not necessarily predominant" contributing cause of your condition. If you lied about your physical condition to get a job, you could be denied benefits. The law says this can happen if you suffer an injury related to that pre-existing medical condition, and you knew or should have known that it was unlikely you could do the job without injuring yourself seriously (M.G.L. Ch. 152, Sec. 27A). If you tell the employer the truth after being hired, and the employer continues to employ you, then you have a right to compensation.

Examples of Occupational Disease

Repetitive motion disorders: Typing and other repetitive work can lead to repetitive motion disorders. Meat cutters, postal workers, secretaries, reporters, nurses, truck and bus drivers are among those susceptible. These disorders include carpal tunnel syndrome, thoracic outlet syndrome, back injuries, tendonitis and "tennis elbow."

Lung disease: Workers exposed to dust, such as in coal mining or weaving and cutting cotton, may develop lung disease. Asbestos, cotton dust, coal, talc and other substances can cause lung cancer, emphysema, chronic bronchitis, talcosis and heart disease. Coal miners have developed "black lung" from a buildup of coal dust in their lungs. Workers who become sensitized to a chemical may develop asthma and reactive airway lung disease. The symptoms may continue after they leave the workplace because the original exposure causes them to become sensitive to other chemicals. Workers who breathe in asbestos particles can develop asbestosis, lung and stomach cancer, and mesothelioma (cancer of the lining of the lungs and body cavity). Asbestosis may take five to 25 years to develop after exposure.

Chemical Illness: Toxic chemicals can make you sick when you breathe them, absorb them through your skin or eat them. You can be exposed to a large dose at once or to smaller doses over a longer period. You may react immediately or after a long time. Some people develop multiple chemical sensitivity and become ill when exposed to common chemicals, such as perfumes, paint, tobacco smoke or gasoline.

Reproductive health hazards: Lead, radiation, ethylene oxide, some solvents and infectious agents (such as rubella) can damage the male or female reproductive system, a developing fetus or a child.

Heart Attacks: If you had pre-existing heart disease, then your job must be "a major cause" for you to receive benefits. If you have a heart attack off the job, you would have to show that symptoms began at work, were brought on by your job and continued until you had the heart attack.

Are mental or emotional impairments covered?

Collecting comp for emotional problems is difficult. You may not have a problem if your condition is due to an obvious incident, such as harassment or violence. The law states, "Personal injuries shall include mental and emotional disabilities only where the predominant contributing cause of such disability is an event or series of events occurring within any employment" (M.G.L. Ch. 152, Section 1). The law also states, "No mental or emotional disability arising principally out of a bona fide, personnel action including a transfer, promotion, demotion, or termination except such action which is the intentional infliction of emotional harm shall be deemed to be a personal injury within the meaning of this chapter" (M.G.L. Ch. 152, Sec. 1).

What if you think the injury was your fault?

You are entitled to benefits no matter who was at fault. In 1911, Massachusetts created a no-fault workers comp system. Workers no longer had to prove employer negligence, but they lost the right to sue their employers for pain and suffering. The law has rare exceptions. You may not get benefits if your "serious and willful misconduct" caused your injury. Similarly, in cases where you can prove that your injury was the result of your employer's "serious and willful misconduct," you may apply for double compensation. (You still will not be able to sue your employer.) Your employer, not the insurer, will have to pay the extra money.

CHAPTER 3

REPORTING YOUR INJURY

I was frightened of filing a claim, even though it was exactly what the personnel manual said you should do. I had heard horror stories about workers comp. I was afraid my employer would become angry with me.

After you have determined that you have a workers comp claim, the next step is to report your injury. The formal process for reporting injuries is explained in this chapter.

How long do you have to report an injury?

You have four years from the date of your injury to file a claim. If you did not know that you had an injury or illness that could be compensated, the four years start when you first become aware.

How do you report an injury?

Tell your employer as soon as possible, even if you can continue to work. The worst pain from your injury may not come immediately. If you have been exposed to hazardous chemicals, report it even if you have no immediate symptoms. If your employer has an accident form to fill out, make sure it is completed and that you get a copy. If you are a union member, inform your union representative. Send a letter to your employer by certified mail, return receipt requested. Describe the location, time and date of the injury and the names of witnesses. If you do not report the injury in writing, your employer may claim that you never reported it.

Your employer has seven days (not including Sundays or legal holidays) after you have been disabled for five days to send FORM 101 (First Report of Injury) to you, the insurer and the DIA. The seven days start *after* you have been unable to work for five calendar days. If you do not report the injury until after the first five days, the report must be filed within seven days of the day the injury was reported. The five days involves all calendar days, including the weekend. The day you get injured counts if you missed four hours or more of work. The five days do not have to be in the same week or consecutive. In the state's fiscal year 2006, (from July 1, 2005, to June 30, 2006) 36,590 first reports of injury were filed with the DIA. In fiscal year 2005, 37,461 first reports of injury were filed with the DIA. In the previous fiscal year, 2004, the number was 36,739.

You will receive an informational brochure from the DIA giving an overview of the system. Keep your copy of the First Report of Injury. If you are not sure your employer has filed the form, contact the DIA Claims Administration at 800-323-3249, ext. 301. If the First Report of Injury is filed late, the DIA can fine your employer. Report the injury yourself to the insurer if your employer has not reported it. The name and contact information for the insurer should be posted in your workplace. If you are unable to find the information, call the DIA.

If you have personal resources at all whatsoever, anyone you could go live with for a year, and your injury is sort of at the medium level, not horrible yet; if you can afford to take a year off and don't deal with workers comp or disability, you're going to be a lot better off psychologically. If you can afford to do that. I realize most of the population can't do that. There is not much advice to give. Once you're in the system, it's kind of out of your control.

----◆----

I was afraid that I would never get promoted if I filed a workers comp claim. I worked in pain for about two years before ever seeing a doctor.

What are the consequences of not reporting an injury?

With all the attention given to fraud, it may come as a surprise that many workers are afraid to report their injuries and get involved with workers comp. They worry that they will be fired, or that their employer will retaliate. Some injured workers have heard about the delays in getting medical treatment and would prefer to be treated under their personal health insurance.

These fears may be legitimate. The decision to file a claim is up to you, but consider the following facts. Your personal health insurer will likely refuse to pay for treatment for a work-related injury. This information will be included in the doctor's notes and forwarded to the insurer if you describe how the injury happened. If you do obtain medical treatment for your injury under your personal health insurance, what will happen if your condition deteriorates and you are unable to work? You will be unable to collect weekly benefits unless you file a claim and produce doctor's notes that say your injury is related to work.

The worst cases are those where the worker not only delays reporting the injury, but delays getting medical treatment out of fear of getting involved with workers comp. This often happens in cases of repetitive strain injuries that begin as a mild condition that can be easily ignored. Employees continue to work, injuring themselves further. Many of these workers eventually have to file for comp anyway, but by the time they do, they have done irreversible damage to their bodies.

Protecting Your Interests from the Beginning

Seek reputable counsel as soon as possible because the workers comp system is not friendly to the worker, and you need to take care of yourself, and you need someone to be watching out for you at all times.

Many injured workers make mistakes in the early stages that affect their ability to win their cases. Injured workers do not know their rights. They are not looking for a fight with their employer, so they do not prepare for one. They just want to get better quickly and return to work. Three common mistakes are going to the company doctor, talking to and using the services of a nurse case manager, and not getting legal help.

Being nice is often a strategy used by the insurer. They know that if they were nasty to you from the first phone call, you would be frightened and hire a lawyer. After reporting your injury, you may get a phone call from an adjuster or nurse case manager who seems concerned and helpful. Your employer may have already sent you to a particular doctor or clinic. Nurse case managers are employees of the insurer. Sometimes, they will come to your home or even go into the doctor's office with you. You should know that you have the right to refuse their services, and that their real job is to gather information for the insurer that could hurt your case.

Company doctors are also called "preferred providers." Again and again, injured workers have told us that they thought they had no choice but to be treated by their employers' preferred providers. The law says that if your employer sends you to a preferred provider, you must see that physician once. Then you are free to see a doctor of your choice. As we explain how the system works in future chapters, you will understand how important medical evidence is in a workers comp case. The law puts the burden on you to prove that you are injured, and that work was the cause. Your own statements about your pain and how the injury occurred will not be enough. You will have to produce a doctor's statement that is supportive of your case. Employers send employees to preferred providers for a reason. It is in their best interest to pick your doctor for you.

Many injured workers hesitate to seek legal representation for the same reasons they do not find their own doctor. They do not want a fight with their employers, and they think that getting a lawyer means they are taking an adversarial stance. Some injured workers mistakenly think that getting a lawyer means they are going to sue their employer, something they cannot do if the employer has workers comp insurance. Neither your employer nor the insurance adjuster will explain all of your rights and options. The adjusters know the system inside and out and have handled hundreds or even thousands of cases before yours. They know all the "tricks," while you know nothing about the system. It makes sense to have someone on your side who is knowledgeable. Legal representation is discussed more fully in Chapter 19.

CHAPTER 4

MEDICAL BENEFITS

I used to run three or four miles every day, and now I can't even walk three blocks. In some ways I still haven't accepted it.

You are entitled to all "reasonable and necessary" medical treatment for a work-related injury or illness. Medical benefits may be the only benefits that you receive if you need medical treatment, but are still able to work. Insurers are less likely to hassle individuals who have what is known as a "medical-only" claim than individuals who are out of work. Keep in mind, however, that while your claim may start out as medical-only, you may stop working if your condition deteriorates.

Who decides what is reasonable and necessary?

The insurer makes an initial decision. If you are denied and file a claim, the decision will be that of an administrative judge in the DIA. In addition, a process called *utilization review* is used to determine if medical treatment is reasonable and necessary. In an attempt to control medical costs and prevent unnecessary treatment, the DIA was required by the 1991 "reform" to issue regulations for health care services. These regulations require all insurers to review medical treatment. DIA guidelines set limits on the type and amount of treatment for a particular condition. The guidelines are used by the utilization agents to determine whether the treatment is "reasonable and necessary." Often, it is your doctor's office that submits a request for treatment to utilization review. Your physician must sometimes write a letter requesting a particular treatment and wait for a response.

How does utilization review affect injured workers?

Although created to control costs, utilization review really amounts to another barrier to medical treatment for injured workers. These guidelines limit the costs to insurers by restricting access to medical treatment. They create obstacles and delays to medical care. You may wonder why it takes so long to get medical procedures scheduled. Utilization review is a major reason.

What about mental health treatment?

Many injured workers become depressed. In addition to dealing with your injuries, you have the stress of going through the workers comp system. You may have little or no income for long periods. You may lose contact with friends and co-workers and become isolated. Who wouldn't fall into a depression under these circumstances? Logic and fairness dictate that the insurer should foot the bill for mental health treatment. In reality, however, it may not be in your best interest to file a workers comp claim around emotional issues.

Why not? First of all, insurers resist claims for psychological injuries even more strongly than those for physical injuries. They think approving them will open the floodgates for people suffering stress as a result of work. Secondly, if the insurer pays for mental health treatment, the insurer will have access to the records of the treatment, and probably use them against you. The insurer is also likely to demand (and obtain) records from mental health treatment you had prior to your injury. If a particularly dramatic incident happened at work, such as violence, it is easier for a worker to establish a link between emotional problems and work.

Should you decide not to include emotional injuries in your workers comp claim, you may try to seek treatment under private health insurance, if you still have it. Many people are successful in getting treatment this way, although a private health insurer may reject payment if it is clear that the depression is due only to a work injury. Sometimes, support groups such as the one run by the Alliance for Injured Workers are free. Finding others in the same situation can be helpful in fighting depression. Some hospitals offer free support groups for people with chronic pain. See Chapter 25 for other suggestions on surviving emotionally.

CHAPTER 5

LOST WAGES

Because I support myself, it became a financial hardship. I could have lost my house. So every penny that I got from workers comp I put toward paying my mortgage. I started surveying my house and personal property and thinking what could I sell so that I don't lose my house.

The system was designed to *compensate* workers for lost wages. The 1991 "reform" cut the amount of compensation and reduced the number of years that injured workers could collect certain types of benefits.

When does compensation for lost wages begin?

You are entitled to a check for lost wages after you have missed work for six days or more. It does not have to be six days in a row. The days add up even if you miss a day here and there, as long as all the absences are for the same injury. If you are disabled for five days or fewer, you may still receive medical, loss of function, and disfigurement benefits. You will be paid for the first five days of disability only if you are disabled for 21 calendar days or more. So, if you are out of work for 20 days, you will only be paid for 15 days. If you are disabled for eight days, you will only be compensated for three days.

How much money will you get while out of work?

Compensation is based on your average weekly wage and whether you are considered totally or partially disabled. To calculate your average weekly wage, add up all your earnings (including overtime, commissions, tips, vacation pay and bonuses) from the 52 weeks before your injury. Divide this total by the number of weeks in which you earned more than $5. Subtract the weeks you were sick, if you were out for more than two weeks.

Fringe benefits such as your employer's contribution to health insurance or your pension plan are not usually counted as part of your average weekly wage, unless wages were subject to "prevailing wage" laws. If you worked for your employer only a short time, the wages earned by an employee engaged at the same work and level will be used to determine an average weekly wage. If you worked two jobs, and your injury at one job prevents you from working at the second job, your total earnings from both jobs will be used to calculate your average weekly wage.

How will your average weekly wage be used to determine your weekly check?

If you cannot perform any work, you are considered temporarily totally disabled. Your disability may, in fact, turn out to be permanent. Nevertheless, this is the category to which you will be initially assigned. Later, it may be possible for you to apply for permanent, total disability. Your weekly check will be 60 percent of your gross average weekly wage. (Prior to 1991, the amount was 66 percent. This is one example of how the "reform" hurt injured workers.) Workers comp benefits are not taxable.

The state sets a maximum and minimum comp benefit based on the state average weekly wage. It is adjusted on October 1 of every year. As of October 1, 2008, the maximum weekly comp benefit was $1,093.27, and the minimum was $218.65. You would be eligible for the minimum if you earned less than 20 percent of the state average weekly wage. The DIA website (www.mass.gov/dia) lists the new amount each year. High-wage earners are particularly hurt by the maximum benefit rate. *Note: You cannot receive benefits while you have outstanding default, arrest warrants or are incarcerated.*

How long can you collect temporary total disability benefits?

You can collect temporary total disability benefits for a maximum of three years (156 weeks). Temporary total disability benefits were reduced from five years (260 weeks) to three years (156 weeks) as part of the 1991 "reform."

What if you are still unable to work after temporary total disability runs out?

Four months before your temporary comp benefits run out, you should file a claim for either "total and permanent disability" or "partial disability." You may be able to receive workers comp for the rest of your life if you are totally and permanently disabled from performing all meaningful, gainful work. Your benefits will be equal to two-thirds of your average weekly wage up to the maximum rate. After two years, you may also be entitled to cost-of-living adjustments. In deciding whether you are permanently and totally disabled, a judge will look at your age, education, training, job experience, and physical limitations.

What are partial disability benefits?

You may find that a judge or the insurer finds you only partially disabled, even if you are out of work altogether. In theory, partial disability benefits were designed for injured workers whose injuries permit them to work but prevent them from earning their full average weekly wage. The reality is that you may find yourself designated as only partially disabled even though your injury prevents you from working at all. In cases of partial disability, you are entitled to compensation even if you did not lose any days from work. You could be eligible for benefits to pay part of your lost wages, if you had to cut your hours, switch to a light duty job *that paid less*, work overtime to make your pre-injury wages or work at a slower pace and lose incentive pay.

If you have been receiving temporary total disability benefits, a judge may reduce these benefits to partial if the judge believes you have the capacity to earn some wages. This will substantially affect the amount of money you will receive as well as the number of years you can collect. The judge or the insurer will assign you an "earning capacity," which is an amount of money that you are supposedly capable of earning. Your comp rate will be 60 percent of the *difference* between your average weekly wage before the injury and the weekly wage you are deemed capable of earning after the injury. No matter how little your earning capacity, the maximum temporary partial disability benefits cannot exceed 75 percent of your temporary total disability benefit. If you are truly only partially disabled, and can make a transition to another career, this category has some logic to it. Some injured workers placed in this category, however, feel that the system does not recognize the severity of their condition. If they are unable to return to work, they sometimes have to turn to other sources of income, such as Social Security disability.

How long do partial disability benefits last?

Partial disability benefits last only five years (260 weeks) unless you have already received temporary total disability benefits. You can only earn benefits under "temporary total disability" and "partial disability" for a combined total of seven years. Partial disability benefits were reduced from 11½ years to five years as part of the 1991 "reform." The law says that partial disability benefits may be extended up to 520 weeks (10 years) if there is a permanent loss of 75 percent of function of a part of your body or one of your senses, a permanently life-threatening physical condition, or a permanently disabling job-related disease.

> *They told me I was only partially disabled, but there was no way I could have worked at any job at that point. My weekly check was about $250.*

----◆----

> *Financially, it was horrendous. I lost my condo. It was devastating. I had bought a condo on my own after my divorce and was able to sustain it and raise my daughter. I was really proud of that. Because of one day, one slip, that went down the tube.*

How does returning to work affect your comp rate?

If you go back to work after receiving comp for your initial injury and have worked for more than two months before getting hurt again, you will be compensated based on your average earnings at the time of your re-injury. This will be true whether or not the subsequent injury is a recurrence of the former injury. (If you received a lump sum benefit, you only receive compensation if it is a new injury.)

CHAPTER 6

DISFIGUREMENT AND LOSS OF FUNCTION

I get angry, defensive. You don't know my work ethic. If I could, I would be working. Don't make a judgment about me because you don't know anything about me. People who knew nothing about me were making decisions about my life.

If your injury results in scarring (disfigurement) or permanent loss of function of a body part or sense, you are entitled to a payment in addition to your weekly compensation. The state has set rates covering every part of your body. In our opinion, the rates are too low. Furthermore, thanks to the 1991 "reform," the only scars that count are those on your face, neck or hands. These are the DIA guidelines for scar-based disfigurement benefits and loss of function. The maximum for scarring is $15,000. "SAWW" stands for State-wide Average Weekly Wage, determined each year on October 1 by the DIA (On October 1, 2008 it was $1,093.27). "Linear scar" means a fine, narrow scar, and "discoloration" means skin color has changed. "Major" is the side of the body you favor. For example, if you are right-handed, your right hand is your "major" hand.

DIA guidelines for scar-based disfigurement benefits and loss of function

Disfigurement

Face

Linear, no discoloration	2 x SAWW per inch
Linear, with discoloration	3.25 x SAWW per inch
Wide, no discoloration	3.5 x SAWW per inch
Wide, with discoloration	6.5 x SAWW per inch

Neck

Linear, no discoloration	1 x SAWW per inch
Linear, with discoloration	1.5 x SAWW per inch
Wide, no discoloration	1.75 x SAWW per inch
Wide, with discoloration	2 x SAWW per inch

Hand

Linear, no discoloration	1 x SAWW per inch
Linear, with discoloration	1.75 x SAWW per inch
Wide, no discoloration	2 x SAWW per inch
Wide, with discoloration	2.5 x SAWW per inch

Loss of function

Arms and Hands

Major arm	43 x SAWW
Shoulder	60% of (43 x SAWW)
Elbow	65% of (43 x SAWW)
Minor arm	39 x SAWW
Shoulder	60% of (39 x SAWW)
Elbow	65% of (39 x SAWW)
Both arms	96 x SAWW
Both hands (at wrist)	77 x SAWW
Major hand	34 x SAWW
Thumb	40% of (34 x SAWW)
Index	25% of (34 x SAWW)
Middle	20% of (34 x SAWW)
Ring	10% of (34 x SAWW)
Little	5% of (34 x SAWW)
Minor hand	29 x SAWW
Thumb	40% of (29 x SAWW)
Index	25% of (29 x SAWW)
Middle	20% of (29 x SAWW)
Ring	10% of (29 x SAWW)
Little	5% of (29 x SAWW)

Legs and Feet

1 Leg	39 x SAWW
Knee	50% of (39 x SAWW)
Hip	25% of (39 x SAWW)
Both legs	96 x SAWW
Either foot (above ankle)	29 x SAWW
Both feet (above ankles)	68 x SAWW
Large toe	18% of (29 x SAWW)
Other toes	5% of (29 x SAWW)

Spine

100% loss (dorsal, lumbar, sacrum)	32 x SAWW
100% loss (of cervical)	24 x SAWW

Equilibrium

Total loss (of ability to stand)	21 x SAWW

Loss of Organ Function

Kidney (Total loss of one)	16 x SAWW
Lung (Total loss of one)	16 x SAWW
Total loss of spleen	10 x SAWW
Urinary or Bowel, total loss of either	29 x SAWW
Sexual Function (Total loss)	10 x SAWW

Loss of Senses

Taste or Smell (Total loss)	16 x SAWW
Hearing:	
Total loss in one ear	29 x SAWW
Total loss in both ears	77 x SAWW
Eyes:	
Total loss of vision	39 x SAWW
Loss of single binocular vision	39 x SAWW
(or reduction to 20/70 of *one* eye with glasses)	
Total loss of vision	96 x SAWW
(or reduction to 20/70 of *both* eyes with glasses)	

Teeth:	
Loss of each natural tooth	1 x SAWW

Language Comprehension:	
Total loss	32 x SAWW

CHAPTER 7

DEATH BENEFITS

My injury didn't kill me, but the process nearly did. I started thinking about suicide.

Western MassCOSH's slogan is, "Working for a living…Shouldn't mean dying for it." Some workers pay the ultimate price for a work injury. The connection between a death and work may be obvious in some cases and difficult to prove in others. A spouse may be entitled to survivor benefits. When a worker dies at work, the death is presumed to be work-related. The burden is on the insurer to prove that the death was not related to the job. If the death was a suicide, the burden is on those representing the deceased worker to prove that the suicide occurred due to the effects of a job injury, such as a depression.

What benefits are available to survivors?

A spouse and dependent children are entitled to survivor benefits. If your spouse dies from a job-related cause, burial expenses are covered up to $4,000. If you remain unmarried, you are entitled to receive two-thirds of your deceased spouse's average weekly wage (not to exceed the maximum compensation rate) up to a maximum of 250 times the state average weekly wage in effect at the time of the injury or death, plus cost-of-living benefits. (After that, you would have to show you are not fully self-supporting to continue receiving these benefits.) Depending on the weekly compensation rate, you may be entitled to receive $6 for each dependent child. Dependents can include full-time students and physically or mentally incapacitated individuals over 18.

If you remarry, these benefits stop, but dependent children are eligible to receive $60 a week. You are also entitled to your spouse's loss of function and disfigurement benefits if your spouse lived for 45 days after the injury. If the surviving spouse dies, the benefits are divided among the children. If you have an unmarried child under age 18 who dies from a job injury or illness, you can receive survivor benefits if the child lived with you at the time of the injury.

Facts about Occupational Fatalities

In 2005, a total of 5,702 workers died on the job in the United States. The number of men killed was 5,300, and the number of women killed was 402. "Transportation incidents" accounted for 2,480 of the deaths. Falls accounted for 767 deaths. Homicides accounted for 564. Ten years earlier, in 1995, the figure was 6,275. (Source: U.S. Department of Labor, Bureau of Labor Statistics, in cooperation with state, New York City, District of Columbia, and Federal agencies, Census of Fatal Occupational Injuries, March 16, 2007)

In Massachusetts, 75 people died on the job in 2005. Sixty-nine were men, and six were women. The statistics were similar for 2004 and 2003. In 2004, 72 people died; 69 men and three women. In 2003, 73 men and five women died on the job, for a total of 78. (Source: U.S. Department of Labor, Bureau of Labor Statistics, in cooperation with state and federal agencies, Census of Fatal Occupational Injuries.)

CHAPTER 8

THE FIRST SIX MONTHS

In a week or two of being out on workers comp, connect with the injured workers group and start talking to lawyers. At least seeking them out. Once you meet that magic number of weeks, it's not going to be a fun ride. Start socking money away and keeping ahead of your bills. Tap into support systems.

In the last few chapters, we described the benefits that should be available to you. Now, we begin describing the reality of fighting a claim. *Fighting* is exactly what injured workers often have to do. What happens if you report an injury, and the insurer refuses to pay? What if everything has been going smoothly for months, but suddenly you receive a notice in the mail that the insurer will no longer be paying you?

You may think that the insurer will be nice to you because your injury is legitimate, and you have always been hard-working. Maybe you think that insurers only contest cases where they have good reason to suspect fraud. The fact is, you are costing the insurer money. Workers with legitimate, work-related injuries have lost their cases and received little or nothing in benefits.

Many injured workers who thought everything was going smoothly suddenly receive a notice that their benefits will stop. Often, they have no idea why the insurer is doing this. They may not realize that the first 180 days is the "pay-without-prejudice period." It means that the insurer has not accepted responsibility for the claim.

How long will you have to wait for the first check?

The insurer has 14 days from the date it receives the first report of injury from the employer to either start paying or to deny the claim. If you begin receiving checks, do not be fooled into thinking that the insurer cannot turn around and deny your claim in the future.

Can the insurer stop your checks?

As long as the insurer sent your first check on time, it can stop your checks anytime within the first 180 days. The insurer must send you a seven-day notice of termination by certified mail. The latest the notice can be mailed is seven days before the six months ends. (With your written permission, the pay-without-prejudice period can be extended to one year. Be sure to discuss the implications with a lawyer before you sign an extension. It may not be in your best interest.)

Can the insurer cut off your checks after six months?

If the insurer lets six months go by while continuing to pay you, stopping or reducing your checks becomes more difficult, but not impossible. It is the insurer who must file at the DIA in order to get the permission of a judge to stop or reduce your weekly checks. During the months it takes to get to a conference before the judge, the insurer must continue paying you. You can see why it is in the interest of the insurer to cut you off before the six months ends. The insurer may hope that the financial pressure will force you back to work.

Under some limited circumstances, the law allows the insurer to cut off your benefits even after the pay-without-prejudice period ends, without obtaining the permission of a judge. Obviously, the insurer can stop your benefits if you return to work or a time limit for a certain type of benefit, such as five years for partial disability, has expired. The insurer can also cut off your benefits if your own doctor or an impartial medical examiner says that you are able to work. (An impartial medical examiner is a physician appointed by the court. We will explain more about impartial medical examiners later.) If your own doctor specifies that you can work with certain restrictions, and your employer offers a "light-duty" job that meets those restrictions, the insurer can cut off your benefits if you refuse to do the job. This points out the importance of medical evidence in workers comp cases and why you should not go to the company doctor. Even finding your own doctor is no guarantee that you and the doctor will agree on whether or not you should be back at work, however.

___

CHAPTER 9

YOUR DAYS IN COURT: CONCILIATION, CONFERENCE AND HEARING

I would change the fact that they don't consider any other doctor's information, any other specialist, but they only take that one doctor who saw me maybe for five minutes over the doctor who saw me for years.... He just asked me a couple of things and then left. I wasn't even in there four minutes, and my whole future depended on that doctor's visit.

In Massachusetts, the government agency that resolves disputed workers comp cases is the Department of Industrial Accidents (DIA). The main office is in Boston, but there are regional offices in Fall River, Springfield, Lawrence and Worcester. The DIA has its own judges who make decisions regarding workers comp cases. If you are denied benefits, you have the right to file a claim at the DIA. Usually, this is done with the help of a lawyer. This begins a process that includes several steps and takes many months. A conciliation is the first step in resolving a disputed case. It may be followed by a conference and a hearing.

What triggers a conciliation?

If the insurer has cut off your benefits or never paid you benefits, you or your lawyer can file a claim at the DIA. On the other hand, if it is the insurer seeking permission to stop or reduce your benefits, the insurer can file a claim. Either way, you will receive a notice in the mail telling you that you have to appear for a conciliation at a certain time and date. You will appear with your lawyer before a conciliator. You may also want to bring a relative or friend for emotional support.

> *When I first got a letter that I had to go to that conciliation meeting, I thought I did something wrong. I felt guilty. I felt almost like belittled and not trusted. That I had to prove that I was in pain and that I got hurt at work. The x-ray showed it. This was all foreign to me, and my first goal when I went out of work was to get better and to feel better, to get back to normal and get back to work. It was almost like they were saying, "You're lying."*

What happens at a conciliation?

Often, the conciliation is over quickly. Your lawyer will speak briefly about your medical condition, and the insurer's lawyer will state why the insurer wants to deny your claim. You may be asked a few questions, or you may say nothing. The conciliator writes a report and makes a recommendation regarding benefits.

What happens after a conciliation?

A conciliation is supposed to be an opportunity for both sides to come to agreement without the case having to go any further. If the insurer does not voluntarily agree to pay you benefits, the conciliator cannot force the insurer to do so. You may have gone several months with no income waiting for the conciliation. Now, you will have to wait several more months to get to the next stage, a conference.

Prior to the conference, arbitration may be an option. If both you and the insurer agree, you can take your case to an arbitrator who will make a final and binding decision. A conference would then be unnecessary. Written notice of this agreement must be given to the DIA at least five days before your conference, using a form called "Agreement to Refer a Case to Arbitration." The arbitrators are not DIA employees. You and the insurer can use the Board of Conciliation and Arbitration, a state agency, or a private arbitration services. Both sides must agree on the choice of the arbitrator. In reality, few cases are taken to arbitration, perhaps because of the difficulty of getting both sides to agree to this option.

What is a conference?

The conference is more formal than a conciliation. You will appear before an administrative judge. Unlike a conciliator, the judge does have the power to order the insurer to pay you. Attending the conference may be difficult. Generally, you do not give testimony. You have to sit quietly while the lawyers for each side make arguments to the judge. You may have a hard time listening to what the lawyer for the insurer says about you.

The reports from your treating physician will play an important role at this stage. Your lawyer will present medical reports from your doctor to substantiate the severity of your injury and the fact that it was caused by work. Again, note the importance of having medical evidence to support your claim. The lawyer for the insurer may point out to the judge weaknesses in your medical evidence. In addition, the insurer may have medical evidence of its own. By this time, the insurer may have sent you to an independent medical examiner (IME). This is a doctor hired by the insurer to examine you and write a report. Often, these doctors write reports that are helpful to the insurer, not to you.

Will the judge make a decision at the conference?

The judge weighs the evidence and makes a decision within seven days of the conference. You will receive a copy in the mail. The judge's order will require or deny benefits or modify or deny modification of benefits. (Modification is usually a request by the insurer to reduce your benefits on the grounds that you are only partially disabled.) You will receive retroactive benefits if the insurer stopped your benefits or never started paying you.

What if you lose at the conference?

If you lose at the conference, you must appeal to get to a hearing. The fee is $450. Sometimes you are required to pay this fee. Sometimes your lawyer will pay it up front, but expect to be reimbursed later. If you have financial hardship, you can request that the DIA waive the fee.

What is it like to go through this process?

You may go for many months with no income. It is difficult to deal with your medical condition, but now you have financial pressures as well. You may be confused and angry, and start to suffer from anxiety and depression. It is ironic that your coworkers may think that you are enjoying a "vacation." You can make a request to the DIA that the conference be scheduled sooner due to hardship, medical emergency or catastrophic injury. Contact the DIA for more information about this option.

Suppose out of desperation, you file for unemployment benefits. This can be used against you since the application asks if you are able to work. Some judges will be understanding of the fact that you needed the income, but some judges may not. Discuss this option with your lawyer. (If at some point, you are awarded partial disability benefits, you may be able to collect unemployment benefits, but the unemployment will be reduced. The insurer may *require* an injured worker receiving partial disability benefits to apply for unemployment.)

What if you win at the conference?

Perhaps everything has gone your way up to this point. You found your own doctor. His or her reports link your medical condition to work and support your need to be out of work. The judge at the conference believed you, and ordered the insurer to pay you. The checks are coming again. The insurer will probably appeal, pushing the case to a hearing. But why should you be worried about that? Your case was solid and strong enough to prevail at the conference. Why should the hearing be any different? In fact, it could be very different.

How is a hearing different from a conference?

The game changes considerably when you get to the hearing. Your own treating doctor's opinion, so important up to this point, now becomes much less important. A very important step happens prior to the hearing. You will receive a letter informing you of the time and date of an impartial medical exam. Failure to go could mean a suspension of benefits.

What is an impartial medical examiner?

The language is confusing, but an *impartial* medical examiner is not at all the same as the *independent medical examiner* hired by the insurer. The impartial physician is chosen by the judge from a roster of physicians approved by the DIA. This impartial medical exam was created by the 1991 "reform." In theory, the impartial exam is supposed to provide an opinion from an objective third party.

You will see the impartial physician once for what may be a very brief exam. The impartial physician will then write a report, answering several questions. Do you have a disability? Is the disability total or partial, permanent or temporary? Was your work a major or predominant contributing cause? Has there been any loss of function? Has a medical end result been reached? The impartial medical examiner will receive and review copies of your physician's reports and the report from the independent medical examiner, if any. Nevertheless, the impartial physician is free to disagree with your treating doctor.

At the hearing, the report from the impartial physician will be the *only medical evidence* allowed. In fact, the 1991 law is written so that the judge is obligated to rely heavily on the report of the impartial physician. The opinion of your own physician, who may have been seeing you for months or years, no longer matters. The impartial physician who saw you once will play a major role in deciding the outcome of your case.

This is one of the worst aspects of the Massachusetts workers comp law. The judge who ruled in your favor at the conference may write a completely different opinion after reading the impartial physician's report. The law states that the issues must be decided at the hearing without any regard to what happened at the conference. You will probably be able to obtain a copy of the impartial physician report from your lawyer prior to the hearing. Discuss with your lawyer the implications for your case.

It's a joke. Someone you don't know who knows nothing of you takes all of, if you're lucky 20 minutes, and makes a decision that's going to affect the rest of your life. God forbid you should go when you're actually at a good time of day. They don't believe you. They think you're faking. How can it be impartial? I would like to see your own doctor have more input rather than having the input of someone who sees you for all of 20 minutes or half an hour.

If your impartial physician writes a report that you believe does not reflect the true extent of your injuries, you may be devastated. For the lawyers and judges, your case is just one among hundreds handled every year. For you, it is a major event in your life. You may not understand how the impartial physician could write such a report. You did nothing wrong. Unfortunately, the system gives this one report a great deal of weight. Have someone with you, a friend or relative, when you read the report, since you may be upset by its content. Then contact your lawyer to find out his or her opinion of the report.

Is there a way to challenge the impartial report?

Your lawyer can try to argue that the report is inadequate or the medical issues in your case are complex. If the judge agrees, this could open the door for additional medical evidence to be submitted. A medically complex case could be one where a pre-existing condition is aggravated by a work injury, the medical condition develops years after the work exposure (such as lung disease), or the worker suffers from several medical problems as a result of the injury. An example of an inadequate report is one that expands the medical issues in your case rather than narrowing them. That means that the impartial report should resolve the issues disputed between your own treating physician and the independent medical examiner hired by the insurer. If the impartial physician's report is even more unfavorable than the independent medical examiner's report, it may be deemed inadequate.

Another way to challenge the impartial physician's report is through a deposition. This is usually done after the hearing, but before the judge makes a decision. Your lawyer questions the doctor about the report, and the answers are additional evidence that can be considered by the judge. If the impartial report is favorable to you, the lawyer for the insurer is likely to depose the impartial physician.

What will happen at the hearing?

The hearing is a trial. You will be called to testify. You may have witness-es testify, also. You will be cross-examined by the lawyer for the insurer. Lawyers for both sides will make arguments to the judge. The judge will be the same one that you had at your conference. The decision will come in the mail several weeks or months after the hearing.

The judge was nice, and I think he was fair. I really do... The judge kept say-ing, "I would love to give you more."

◆

I felt demeaned by what the judge said. The bias came through. Clearly, the judge thought that people in my situation were a little bit lazy and needed to be pushed back to work. I loved my job and would have been working if I could have been.

◆

That was horrific. I had to hand control over my destiny to people who didn't know me. They didn't want to hear of my present struggle, and they could be making decisions that would affect my survival. Will I have a roof over my head? Will I ever get better? I really can't go back into my career... Everyone told me I had the toughest judge, even my lawyer. Even though, yes, she has a job to do, she admitted to me that if I didn't settle she was going to lower my weekly workers comp benefit to $88 a week...I felt like she didn't want to hear the details, the boohoos. None of that mattered. It sounded like she wasn't working for the injured workers. She was more for the insurer.

What is the role of the judge?

The notice you receive in the mail of a conference date will include the name of the judge assigned to your case. This is important because some judges are more sympathetic to injured workers than others. Ask your lawyer or other injured workers about the judge's reputation. To some extent, the judge's hands are tied because of the impartial physician report. Still, we believe that judges can be influenced by preconceived ideas.

Judges do not fall into these positions by accident. They are appointed by the governor with the approval of the Governor's Council. Few citizens pay much attention to the Governor's Council election. The Alliance for Injured Workers has met with candidates for the Governor's Council and explained the importance of appointing judges who understand issues facing the disabled. Furthermore, administrative judges in the DIA are reappointed every six years. You have the right to attend a meeting of the Governor's Council and speak for or against reappointment of a judge. You can also contact your representative on the Governor's Council privately.

Injured workers often ask if they can have their case assigned to a different judge. The law states, "Except where events beyond the control of the department makes such scheduling impracticable, the administrative judge assigned to any case referred to the division of dispute resolution shall retain exclusive jurisdiction over the matter and any subsequent claim or complaint related to the alleged injury shall be referred to the same administrative law judge" (M.G.L. Ch. 152, Sec. 10A).

Is there an appeals process?

If you lose at the hearing stage, you can appeal to the Reviewing Board. You must file the appeal within thirty days after the hearing decision is filed. You will have to wait about two years for a decision. The board does not retry your case or decide if the judge made the "right" decision. The board will reverse the hearing judge's decision only if it was "beyond the scope of his authority, arbitrary or capricious, or contrary to law" (M.G.L. Ch. 152, Sec. 11C). Decisions made by the Reviewing Board are posted on the DIA website. This is public information. This means that your name, medical information and case history will be posted. If you lose at the reviewing board stage, you can appeal to the Massachusetts Court of Appeals.

How will you survive if you lose your case?

The law puts the burden of proving your case on you, but you are in no position to "prove" a legal case within a system about which you know nothing. Even the injured worker who becomes knowledgeable about the system early and takes all the right steps has limited control over how the case will be resolved. Please know that you are not alone. Later chapters of this book offer suggestions on how to survive under the circumstances. At the Alliance for Injured Workers, we accept and advocate for workers who have lost their cases just as we do for workers who have won their cases. Those who have lost are often in greater need of help.

CHAPTER 10

SETTLING YOUR CASE

*I was just mortified that I went through all that, and it could be so little.
And I got a lot compared to a lot of people.*

You have probably heard that some injured workers receive a lump sum
settlement, but you may be unsure what that means. Injured workers
cannot sue their employers, so a workers comp settlement is not like a
settlement in an automobile accident or a product liability case. You cannot collect damages for pain and suffering.

Between 7,000 and 8,000 workers comp settlements have been approved each year for the last several years, according to the Department
of Industrial Accidents. For the state's fiscal year of 2005, the figure was
7,107, and in the previous fiscal year, 2004, it was 7,962.

Only you can decide whether or not you should settle. Many injured
workers agonize over this decision. Some vow that they will never settle,
thinking that settlements are in the best interest of the insurer. Others
mistakenly think that they are "entitled" to a settlement because other
injured workers have received them.

What is a lump sum settlement?

A settlement is an agreement negotiated between you and the insurer.
Both parties have to be willing to settle. A settlement would mean the
end of weekly checks, but not necessarily the end of payment for medical treatment. Under the 1991 law, a settlement cannot occur without

the approval of your employer. That means that your employer's workers comp insurance company cannot settle with you on its own, without involving your employer.

At what stage are cases settled?

The timing of the settlement varies. Occasionally, a case is settled very early. More often, cases are settled after the impartial physician has submitted a report and before the hearing. You may go to court expecting to testify at your hearing and find that the insurer has made a settlement offer. You will not have much time to make a decision. Occasionally, cases are settled after the hearing. For example, an injured worker who wins total and permanent disability benefits may decide after several years to accept a settlement rather than continue receiving weekly checks.

How can you settle when you still need medical treatment?

A settlement does not necessarily mean that the insurer will stop paying medical bills. In many settlements, the insurer is still responsible (for the rest of your life) for medical bills related to the work-related injury. These are referred to as "accepted" cases because the insurer has accepted liability.

Cases settled without a continuation of medical benefits are called "unaccepted." Be sure you discuss with your lawyer and understand the terms of your settlement. Even in unaccepted cases, a sharp deterioration of your injury that could not have been foreseen could still open the door for payment of medical expenses.

Of course, the continuation of medical benefits does not mean the end of hassles. The insurer will be required to pay only for treatment considered "reasonable and necessary," and utilization review will still be in effect. The insurer can continue sending you to independent medical examiners, and take you back to court to argue that your medical treatment is neither reasonable nor necessary. You may have to take the insurer back to court to collect reimbursement for prescriptions and mileage.

How much of your settlement will your lawyer take?

If the case is accepted, your lawyer will take 20 percent. If the case is unaccepted, the lawyer will take 15 percent. The lawyer cannot take a percentage of a payment for loss of function or disfigurement. Liens could be placed on your settlement by the Department of Transitional Assistance or the Division of Medical Assistance if you have received welfare benefits or MassHealth. Private health insurers who have paid for treatment related to your work injury may also seek to be reimbursed out of your settlement. Overdue child support payments may be deducted.

Should you settle?

We have seen injured workers refuse to settle, go through a hearing, receive a favorable judgment and collect benefits for many years. We have also seen injured workers turn down settlements, then lose their cases and get nothing. Clearly, there is no easy way to decide what the right choice is for you.

There are advantages to settling in some cases. You know how much money you are getting. You take the decision out of the hands of a judge. If you settle before a hearing, you can avoid the hearing altogether. You will not have to testify or be cross-examined. Even injured workers who receive settlements that they believe are unfair often experience a sense of relief. They no longer have to fight the insurer or worry about surveillance.

How do you decide if the settlement offer is fair?

First of all, you must realize that the concept of fairness does not really enter into the equation. This is unfortunate, but true, and if you are waiting for an offer that truly compensates you for all you have lost, you probably will never see it.

Consider, for example, injured workers who are designated as only partially disabled. These benefits last only five years. You may have a serious disability that will make it difficult or impossible for you ever to return to regular, full-time work. Yet, you only qualify for partial disability benefits.

Although I knew I deserved a far greater settlement than I received, I couldn't risk going into a courtroom, and having a biased judge who did not agree with the seriousness of my injury and with my inability to work. I would have walked out of that courtroom with nothing. The judge told me, "You've done well." That was her opinion. If I'm not able to return to work for the rest of my life, that money is not going to do much for me in a 30- or 40-year span.

…After settling, I felt a sense of relief that people weren't sitting in front of my house and following me around in their car, following me on vacation. Yeah, it's a huge sense of relief to know that your life isn't going to be interfered with in that way.

◆

I felt some relief, but there was also disappointment, depression, because it was so far less than what I thought it should be...Even though to me she [the judge] seemed more sympathetic than what I heard of her reputation, it was still devastating. I was just too emotionally upset and crying to understand.

----◆-----

With the settlement I was in such an emotional place to make such a big decision and was just totally out of control. Then having to make that decision right then and there. Do you want to settle, or do you want to pursue it? Extreme pressure. It was like life and death. It was survival. It wasn't like you were going to settle and get a big chunk of change and take a cruise. I felt powerless. I was under so much emotional stress that I would have done almost anything to get it over with because it was such a nightmare.

----◆----

I had gone that day thinking I would have to testify, not even aware of what a settlement meant. I had to make up my mind that morning. As bad as it was, within a month or two, I started to feel relieved. Although I would have to live with the injury for the rest of my life, the workers comp case was behind me.

The insurer will calculate how much you would receive in weekly checks in the time remaining before the five years end. Certainly, the settlement offer will not exceed this amount and probably will be less. Therefore, the offer may seem inadequate and unfair, but the insurer has no incentive to offer more. Prior to 1991, partial disability benefits lasted 11½ years, and settlement offers were much larger.

Add the impartial physician report into the equation. Was it favorable toward you, unfavorable, or somewhat in the middle? If it was unfavorable, the insurer may make a low settlement offer or none at all. The insurer has a good chance of winning before a judge, and not having to pay you anything.

What if you are offered only a very small settlement?

Imagine yourself in the worst possible situation. The impartial medical examiner's report is unfavorable. Your lawyer advises you that your chances of winning before the judge in the hearing are slim. The insurer is offering only a small settlement, basically to avoid the hassle and expense of a hearing. You have the option of having your lawyer depose the impartial medical examiner. The deposition may make your case stronger, or it may not. Your lawyer can try to have the judge declare the impartial physician's report inadequate.

The dilemma you face is whether it is better to risk getting nothing from a hearing or take a settlement that is not much better than nothing. Under these circumstances you may be panicked about how you will survive. You are not well enough to go back to work at any job, and you cannot live for long on the small settlement that is being offered. After working hard for many years, you are also outraged that the impartial physician and the system are not recognizing the true extent of your disability. Regardless of what choice you make, if you are left with no income and no ability to work, there may be other alternatives for you, such as applying for Social Security disability. See Chapter 24 and Chapter 25 for suggestions on how to live with a long-term disability.

Can you return to your old job after settling?

If you settle, there is a presumption that you cannot return to work for the same employer, at least for a certain period of time. For each $1,500 of your settlement, you will be unable to return for one month. For example, if you settled your case for $36,000, then you could not return to the same employer for two years. (The employer can choose to waive this presumption and hire the injured worker earlier.) If you return to work after receiving a lump sum settlement, and then go out of work due to an injury, you cannot receive weekly compensation unless the subsequent claim is determined to be a new injury.

What if you have agreed to a settlement, but are having second thoughts?

Before a settlement is final, it must be approved by a judge or a conciliator. You will be asked whether or not you agree to the settlement. If you express any doubt, the judge or conciliator will not approve the settlement. Many injured workers have mixed feelings at this point. They have decided to settle, but still feel it is unfair. If you want the settlement to be approved, this is not the time to express those reservations.

How will a lump sum settlement affect future Social Security disability benefits?

A settlement will not necessarily interfere with these Social Security disability benefits. There are ways for your lawyer to structure the settlement to prevent or reduce offset of your Social Security benefits. This usually involves presenting the settlement as smaller payments stretched over your expected life span. (You still get the lump sum all at once.) Make sure that your lawyer is aware that you have applied or intend to apply for Social Security disability. You could lose a significant amount of money if this is not handled appropriately.

What happens if you do not settle and win your case?

Chances are, the insurer will continue to hassle you while you collect weekly checks. The insurer will have you followed, send you to independent medical examiners and take you back to court to argue that your condition has improved. Some injured workers do have the fortitude to endure this type of harassment, and they prefer to take the weekly checks rather than settle.

Case History:

Yes, I'm in a wheelchair. But it's not going to keep me down.

This worker was a nurse for more than 30 years. She was working for the state Department of Mental Retardation, inspecting group homes, when she was tripped by a cat kept as a pet by one of the residents at a group home. The fall herniated two discs in her back and damaged her spinal cord. The injury left her unable to walk more than a few steps. She uses a wheelchair. "I can't sit for long, can't stand for long. I'm always moving to get comfortable. If I stay on my feet, my back just buckles. I hit the floor. It's happened a couple of times."

Like many other injured workers with permanent injuries, she assumed she would recover and return to work. "I told everyone, 'Oh, no. This is only temporary. I'm going back to work.' Who wants to think that at my age I'm going to be totally disabled in a wheelchair?"

She went for a long period with no income. "Nothing and nothing for over a year." Each doctor she went to gave the same prognosis. She was permanently and totally disabled. "I wasn't thrilled because I am a workaholic. I did not want to be retired. I did not want to be in a wheelchair or disabled." Doctors offered no cure, only medication to control the pain. "I take my Oxycodone morning and night and during the day if I need to."

She thinks the nature of her injury made it easier for her to prove her case than it is for injured workers with invisible injuries. "It's easier for me. I don't have a disability that doesn't show. I come wheeling up and you know damn well there's something wrong with me." Nevertheless, when her case went before a judge at the DIA, the lawyer for the state aggressively fought her disability claim. (The employer, the state, was self-insured.) The lawyer tried to blame her weight. She testified that she had gained a great deal of weight after becoming disabled because she was much more sedentary.

The judge asked her if she could walk. "I said, 'Yes, short distances, but yeah, I do. I have chairs set up all around the house. I do a few steps and sit. I do a few steps and sit. I can take a few steps.'" She soon learned why the question was asked. The lawyer for the state had a videotape of her walking inside her home. She had been filmed through the windows!

"How the hell did he get pictures of me walking across the room? He said, 'She can walk. She is not disabled.' I teared up. It looked like I was hurt, but I was pissed."

The state offered her a settlement that she thought was too low. Yet, the state was in the midst of a fiscal crisis, and she was told that was all she would be able to get. So, she felt she had no choice but to take it. "The settlement wasn't even a year's pay. $30,000 for an injury like that! I was told, 'You had better take it while you can take it.'" She qualified for state retirement benefits and Social Security disability. (The Social Security checks are reduced as an offset of the state retirement.) Still, she said, "I do not make as much money in a month as I used to make in a week."

This injured worker has fought hard for her independence. She bought a wheelchair van.

"Yes, I'm in a wheelchair," she said. "But it's not going to keep me down."

What can you learn from this case?

- If you are permanently and totally disabled, you may not realize or accept that for a long time.

- Private investigators can be very aggressive, even filming injured workers through windows.

- Be careful not to make absolute statements in court. Had this injured worker said she could not walk at all, the lawyer for the insurer would have tried to make it look as if she were exaggerating.

- Settlements are usually not "jackpots," that allow you to live extravagantly for the rest of your life.

- Even when you win, you may feel as if you have lost.

Case History:

I just miss being who I was before I got injured.

This worker was in good health when she was employed by a temporary agency and sent to work at a company that performs environmental testing. Eventually, she was hired by the company. She occasionally performed clerical tasks, but spent most of her time in the laboratory, handling hazardous chemicals, including methylene chloride, methanol, toluene, and acetone. She recalls that one day the lab was inspected by OSHA. She was tested and found to have been overexposed to some of the chemicals.

"I worked there only six months. I started getting sick from the beginning. My sister kept saying, 'You've got to quit this job.'" In addition to the daily exposure that seemed to be making her chronically ill, a couple of dramatic incidents occurred. "I was doing a well water sample. I was using a lot of methylene chloride, and a large beaker of waste exploded and got absorbed into my stomach." Another time while at work, she said, "I started feeling really shaky, and when I went on break, I started dropping things. Everything started spinning, and I couldn't breathe." She went on her own to an urgent care center and was then sent to the emergency room.

"Outside of work, I was really fatigued and tired all the time. I kept repeating myself twice. I had headaches." Sometimes while driving, she would forget her destination. She became sensitive to common odors, such as perfume, cologne and cleaning powders. She eventually told her employer that she could no longer work in the lab, but asked if she could perform clerical tasks. The company refused.

Her doctors diagnosed her with multiple chemical sensitivity and attributed it to her work in the lab. She was also found to have Hepatitis C, but the cause of it was not clear. She thinks it may have come from her previous work as a medical assistant or from the well water she handled in the lab. She was denied compensation and went for about a year with no income. "I had a really nice car, and the first thing was, it got repossessed."

Still, her case seemed strong. The impartial physician agreed that work exposure to chemicals had triggered multiple chemical sensitivity. The insurer offered a settlement, but her lawyer advised her to reject it. "I thought I had a good case....I thought it would be better to hold out." Her boss testified at the hearing. "The boss said I was sick all the time. Other people testified that they knew I was getting sick. I really thought I was going to win."

The lawyer for the insurer tried to discredit her diagnosis. "She tried to make everything out to be a lie, and that multiple chemical sensitivity isn't really like an illness. Because it's not like diabetes, they don't consider it an illness." After the hearing, the insurer's lawyer deposed the impartial physician. He said that multiple chemical sensitivity is a valid diagnosis, but admitted that it is controversial in the medical community. He said that the worker's Hepatitis C was unrelated to the chemical exposure, but that there was some overlap of symptoms between these conditions. He also said he could not claim within a reasonable degree of medical certainty that the levels of chemicals she was exposed to were sufficient to cause multiple chemical sensitivity.

The judge denied benefits, citing the impartial physician's statements made during the deposition. "I was really depressed. I just couldn't believe it, because I was totally healthy before I took that job." She appealed, a process that took years, but the appeals were denied. "I never got a cent." She has survived over the last 10 years by living on a monthly Social Security disability check that is about $600 a month. She has tried to go back to school to retrain, but feels that her ability to retain information was damaged by the chemicals. She is determined to try to work again. "It's embarrassing. I run into people and they ask, 'What do you do?' I say, 'Oh, nothing, I'm sick.' They say, 'Well, you don't look sick.'"

She said she has become a loner who stays home. "You can go to any public place at any time, and everything is OK, and the next thing you know someone comes by you with perfume, cologne, or hairspray or something. I start getting shaky, and I can't breathe. When I have those bad attacks, I usually end up in bed for three days."

The physical illness and isolation have led to depression. "I have depression, and I never had that before. I just miss being who I was before I got injured."

What can you learn from this case?

- Workers who suffer from illnesses, rather than injuries, have a harder time getting compensation.
- No matter how strong your case seems, turning down a settlement carries a risk of getting nothing.

CHAPTER 11

TRICKS OF THE (INSURANCE) TRADE

I just never thought there would be any question. I had misplaced faith in humanity.

Know your adversary. Insurers are in business to make money. They do not know you and do not care about you. This chapter describes some of the strategies that they use to fight claims.

Why do insurers contest claims?

You may make the mistake of believing that the insurer is only interested in weeding out cases of fraud. There are, in fact, certain circumstances that will raise suspicion. If you report a back injury on Monday, the insurer may wonder if you really injured your back over the weekend. If you are the mother of small children, the insurer may suspect that you want to stay home with them. A history of previous claims may be considered suspicious. The insurer may call your employer to get a sense of how you are regarded as an employee.

But even if none of these circumstances apply to you, the insurer may still contest your case. Insurers are *not* only interested in weeding out cases of fraud. Insurers are interested in paying out as little money as possible. Typically, they will not contest that handful of extreme cases that result in very severe injuries (for example, leaving the worker paralyzed). Otherwise, they have little to lose from contesting your case. You are just one of thousands of cases that they handle, and it is not personal.

To you, it is very *personal*. It involves your career, your health, your reputation, and your ability to buy food and keep a roof over your house.

Why can't you trust an adjuster who seems so friendly?

The adjuster knows that if he or she treated you badly from the beginning, you would probably run to a lawyer's office. So, the strategy is to be nice to you. You get a call from a friendly and sympathetic adjuster. A friendly nurse case manager helps you arrange medical appointments. Your weekly checks start coming. You are not aware of the "pay-without-prejudice" period, or that a nurse case manager serves the interest of the insurer. You think everything is going fine. Like a good employee, you passively do what you are told. You expect to get better and go back to work. Why would you need a lawyer? That is exactly how the insurer wants you to feel.

How do insurers attack claims?

You have a legitimate injury. What possible grounds can the insurer have to contest your claim? Insurers sometimes argue that a claim has no merit or is fraudulent, accusing the worker of faking an injury. Such accusations are rare. Here are some of the more common ways that insurers attack claims:

- Acknowledge that you are injured, but try to claim the injury did not happen as a result of work.

- Argue that you injured yourself outside of work.

- Argue that you have a pre-existing injury. The insurer argues that a car accident you were in several years ago is the real cause of your disability (even though you fully recovered from the accident).

- Argue that some other activity or hobby caused the injury. (Be wary of any forms the insurer sends you requesting information about your hobbies and daily activities. Consult with your lawyer.)

- Argue that your physical problems are the result of some other underlying medical condition. It is not uncommon for injured workers to be told by the company doctor that their pain is caused by arthritis or aging. The insurer might also claim that underlying "psychological" problems are behind your claim.

- Acknowledge that the injury occurred at work, but dispute how disabling the condition is.

- Argue that your injury is not severe enough to require time out of work.

- Argue that you have recovered sufficiently to go back to work.

- Argue that you are able to do some other type of work even if you cannot return to your previous employment.

Of course, in order to make any of these arguments, the insurer has to present evidence. Among the tools at the insurer's disposal are independent medical examiners, private investigators and cross-examination. Private investigators are discussed in the next chapter.

How do independent medical examiners help the insurer?

The independent medical examiner is a doctor hired by the insurer to examine you and write a report. This gives the insurer medical evidence to counter your own physician's report. The independent medical examiner may ask about pre-existing conditions, hobbies and activities outside of work, probing for something other than work that might be a cause of your injury. He or she may accept that work caused your injury, but claim you are ready to go back.

What is the goal of cross-examination?

If you testify at a hearing, the lawyer for the insurer will cross-examine you. The goal will be to attack your credibility. The more absolute your statements are during direct examination, the easier it will be to challenge them during cross examination. If you say, "I can't do anything," the lawyer may respond by asking you about your activities on a typical day.

The insurer's lawyer may try to paint you as a disgruntled employee. People who are unhappy with their jobs may be viewed as having a reason to fake an injury. The lawyer may ask questions to elicit your opinion of your employer. If you respond with an angry tirade, you will be doing just what the other side wants.

Some injured workers feel they must "look" disabled when they go to court. They think that the judge will not believe them unless they show signs of physical distress. This approach can backfire. It may come across as "acting" or exaggerating.

What other tricks do insurers use?

- Starving you out. The insurers understand the financial and emotional stress you are suffering when you go for weeks or months with no income. They want to keep you in this state. They are trying to force you to go back to work or to settle.

- Delaying reimbursement for prescriptions. This creates endless hassles for injured workers who pay up front for medication. You may have to go back to court to get reimbursed. The insurer is hoping that you give up, and some injured workers do.

CHAPTER 12

SURVEILLANCE

You're afraid to live your life with an injury knowing you're being watched like a criminal.

Many of the injured workers that we meet through the Alliance for Injured Workers have been followed by private investigators. Insurers hire them to provide evidence that you are not as disabled as you claim to be. Surveillance can also be used to harass you and induce you to take a settlement.

What are private investigators looking for?

Obviously, they would like to hit the jackpot and catch you collecting while secretly working at a second job. Secondly, they want to catch you engaged in some activity that seems incompatible with your injury, such as water skiing or installing aluminum siding. These are the cases that you hear about in the media. TV news programs will often show the "incriminating" tape.

You may be thinking that you have nothing to worry about because you are not working at a second job, nor engaging in any athletic activity. Private investigators rarely find cases of outright fraud, even though the few cases that occur receive a great deal of publicity. This does not mean that the private investigators go back to the insurers empty handed. They will try to film you doing something that *might* call into question your disability. Are you taking out the garbage, carrying in groceries, mow-

ing the lawn, or working in your garden? You may be doing these things because there is no one else to do them for you. You may also be in pain while or after you do them. The pain will not show on the tape, just the activity.

If the private investigator can film you doing *something*, he or she can present that "evidence" to the insurer. When you go to the DIA, the lawyer for the insurer may show the tape to the judge and argue that you are not as disabled as you claim. Of course, your lawyer may be successful in countering these arguments. Nevertheless, being followed and accused in this fashion can be stressful, particularly when it happens on top of all the stress you are experiencing. You may start to worry every time you leave the house whether or not someone is following you. Just the idea of being followed and observed is disturbing to most people, even if nothing they are doing could be called into question.

What is workers comp fraud?

The extreme is an individual who fakes an injury (or exaggerates the effects of the injury) and "double dips," collecting workers comp while going out every day to another job (sometimes paid under the table). This is fraud and can result in serious criminal penalties. There are also individuals who *are* injured, yet work on the side for a short period, such as one day or a few hours. Maybe someone they know offers to pay them cash to help out on a job. Some injured workers may be tempted by such offers. They need the money and think that their bodies can handle a few hours of work for one day. These injured workers could face suspension of benefits and criminal charges. The law requires an employee receiving weekly comp benefits to report to the insurer "all earnings, including wage or salary from self-employment" (M.G.L. Ch. 152, Sec. 11D).

We believe that even in those cases where an injured worker is "caught" in some type of athletic activity, the videotape is not always conclusive proof of fraud. Some injured workers get bored staying at home, and will attempt for one day an activity they used to do for fun, particularly if it involves muscles other than those that are injured. In-dividuals with chronic pain learn how to conserve their energy, exerting themselves for one day, then resting for several days. The problem is that all that appears on the videotape is the one moment of exertion, not the hours spent lying in bed the next day.

The problem is compounded by the perception of many healthy in-dividuals that if you are injured, you should appear sick at all times. They think that they should be able to *see* you in pain, hobbling along. They expect to see the outward signs of disability, such as canes, neck braces or wheelchairs. If you *look* fine, they are likely to wonder why you are not back at work. They may be resentful that they have to work while you do not, and they do not expect to see you out having fun. We understand and support the need of disabled individuals to get out of their homes and enjoy life. Still, you need to be aware that surveillance videos can be damaging to your case.

A lot of attention is given to fraud by employees. It is important to remember that employers can commit workers comp fraud as well. Em-ployer fraud includes employers who misrepresent the size or nature of their work force to the insurer in order to lower their premiums. An example would be an employer who hides the number of employees engaged in hazardous jobs. This is also called "premium fraud." Some employers may also try to persuade employees to obtain medical treatment under their own health insurance for a work-related injury. Medical providers can commit fraud by ordering unnecessary treatment or billing for a procedure that was not performed.

Is it easy to spot a private investigator?

Many of our injured workers have known when someone has been following them, but others have not, and have been surprised to find out weeks later that a surveillance video exists. Sometimes they do not learn of the existence of these tapes until they go to a conference or hearing at the DIA. We suspect that sometimes private investigators do not care if the injured worker realizes he or she is being followed. The insurer may be using surveillance as a form of harassment. If an injured worker has won total and permanent disability benefits, for example, he or she may be followed repeatedly. Eventually, the injured worker may decide to settle with the insurer rather than endure this harassment. That may be exactly what the insurer wants.

I don't know for sure but I think I was [followed]. My landlord knocked on the door one day and said, "There were two gentlemen here asking questions about you." I remember seeing a white van out on the street for several days in a row. It made me feel cautious, afraid that if I went to put out the trash or walked ten or 15 steps, they would say, "See!"

◆

It's scary as a woman. You assume they are someone from the insurer, but how do you know? Most often they were men.

----◆----

After everything I have been through and all the times I tried to go to work, why are they wasting their money following me? The only reason is to harass me. No way in all honesty they could say I'm faking. So, they're certainly not doing it and realistically thinking they are going to find me out jumping rope...

How aggressive can private investigators be?

Once you leave your home, private investigators are free to film you. It is even legal for them to film you through the windows of your home. They cannot trespass on your land, but if the window blinds or curtains are open, and what you are doing is visible to someone on the street, they can film you. If you are lifting weights near a window, for example, this could be captured on videotape. The investigator may call your home to see if you are there during the day. This is an old technique, but not a particularly useful one today with answering machines and voicemail.

We have heard of some cases where private investigators have crossed the line, in our opinion. This has included investigators going onto private property and looking through windows. Unfortunately, not much has happened when the injured workers reported these incidents to police.

Insurers are torn in two directions. They would love to "catch" you on videotape, but they do not like spending money on private investigators. Insurers will pay for only a limited number of hours of surveillance.

How should you handle being followed?

If you are out of work for a few weeks or months, it may be reasonable to "lay low" for a while, avoiding activities that could be misinterpreted. If you are left with chronic pain and disability, on the other hand, you have a right to have some kind of life. Part of learning to live with chronic pain is developing strategies that allow you to do some of the activities that you enjoy. You may rest for several days before or after doing something strenuous. Doctors and psychologists who work with chronic pain patients often encourage such strategies.

One reason that many injured workers settle is so that they can live their lives without having to worry about their activities being questioned. It is unjust that any injured worker is "pushed" into a settlement, but the reality is that many injured workers feel a great sense of relief after they settle and no longer have to worry about surveillance.

Do's and don'ts for dealing with private investigators:

- Don't confront or threaten the investigator. Your emotions could easily escalate. The investigator will include this in the report. If you strike the investigator not only could you face charges, but the incident will be used as proof of your physical strength.

- Don't work for pay without reporting it, even if it is for only one day or a few hours. You could face criminal charges, and the small number of fraud cases hurt all injured workers.

- Don't stop enjoying life and getting out of your house. Disabled individuals should not be prisoners in their own homes.

- Do consider how some of your activities might be misconstrued or difficult to explain.

- Do call the police if you see a vehicle parked in your neighborhood for several hours or days. If the investigator has not checked in with the police department, an officer may come out and question him or her. You might as well hassle the investigator.

- Do ask a relative to do yard work and shovel snow or pay someone if you can afford it. Obviously, you may not be able to afford to pay someone, and you may not have relatives who can help.

- Do have your doctor put his or her approval in your record for any exercise you are doing. If your doctor advises you to exercise at a gym, be sure that recommendation is documented. Private investigators often think they have struck gold when they "catch" an injured worker working out. Perhaps you take a walk every day. This is probably very good for your body and your recovery. Ask your doctor to mention and recommend it in the notes.

How often are injured workers prosecuted for fraud?

While approximately 37,000 work injuries are reported in the state of Massachusetts each year, only a handful of injured workers are prosecuted for fraud. The following information about 2005 cases is from the Office of the Massachusetts Attorney General, Media Center: http://www.ago.state.ma.us/

- A car dealer was sentenced to serve two years probation and to pay $55,000 in restitution for workers compensation fraud and insurance fraud. According to an investigation, he worked at a used car dealership while collecting workers comp and private disability benefits.

- A Big Dig worker was placed on probation for two years and ordered to pay $10,000 in restitution and perform 136 hours of community service after he pled guilty to workers compensation fraud and larceny over $250. He had filed a claim after injuring his thumb. According to an investigation, he was making renovations to homes while receiving benefits.

- A couple was sentenced to one year under house arrest, followed by four years of probation, and ordered to pay restitution of $55,000 after pleading guilty to workers compensation fraud and larceny over $250. The couple submitted 500 taxi receipts for reimbursement for the man's travel to medical appointments. An investigation concluded that 200 of the receipts were for dates when he had no medical appointments. The cab company named on the receipts had gone out of business in 1998, and the cab driver named on the receipts said that he had not driven the couple to the appointments.

- A former correctional officer was sentenced to two years in the House of Corrections (suspended), 150 hours of community service and ordered to pay restitution of $94,657 for workers compensation fraud and larceny over $250. While receiving benefits for a back injury, he was videotaped performing home improvements.

- After pleading guilty to workers compensation fraud and larceny over $250, a worker was sentenced to serve two and a half years in the House of Corrections, perform 150 hours of community service and pay restitution of $36,466. While receiving benefits for a wrist injury, an investigation revealed that he had opened and ran a grocery store.

- A Big Dig worker pleaded guilty to workers compensation fraud and larceny over $250. He was sentenced to two and a half years in the House of Corrections, 100 hours of community service and payment of $95,405 in restitution. An investigation found that he had been working contracting jobs as a plumber while receiving workers comp for an injury.

- A worker pleaded guilty to workers compensation fraud, larceny over $250 and perjury. He was sentenced to two and a half years in the House of Corrections, two years probation and payment of $137,795 in restitution. An investigation revealed that he had been working for a construction company while receiving workers comp. The perjury charges stemmed from his testimony under oath that he was in severe pain and unable to work.

CHAPTER 13

PUT YOUR HEALTH FIRST

If you have persistent pain that is clearly being made worse by your job, just stop! Just stop working right now. Take time off now. I know I wouldn't have believed that if someone had told me that at the time.

Recovering from your injury and protecting your body from further injury should be your highest priority. Nothing is more important than your health and your body's ability to function. Your ability to work, to care for your family and do the activities you enjoy depends on it.

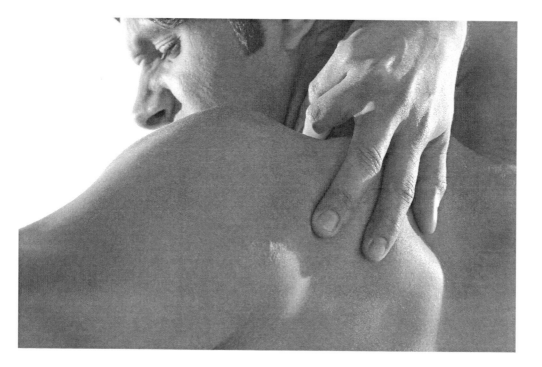

What keeps injured workers from putting their health first?

You may be afraid to report your injury. Some injuries (such as repetitive strain injuries) develop slowly, and it is possible to ignore the pain and continue working, at least for a while. You may be reluctant to take time out of work because your employer will not like it. Financial pressure may push you back to work before you are ready. Perhaps your own doctor does not understand the extent of your pain, and is unwilling to say in writing that you need to be out of work.   We live in a culture where people are admired and praised for being stoic about pain. The athlete who plays the game in spite of an injury is seen as a great team player. Your employer may have policies or practices that discourage the reporting of injuries. But physical pain is not part of anyone's job description. Pain is a signal to stop. Make up your mind that you have a right not to be in pain.

What are the consequences of not putting your health first?

You may not understand how risky it is to continue to injure yourself. Sometimes pain and disability become permanent. If your condition worsens or becomes permanent, you could lose your job anyway, and it may be difficult or impossible to retrain for another profession. Protecting your body is ultimately even more important than keeping your job or winning your workers comp case.

What if you lose your health insurance?

Although the workers comp insurer is supposed to pay for your work-related injury, you might be faced with having no health insurance to cover your other medical problems. Your employer is not required to continue your fringe benefits, including your health insurance, while you are out of work. (Some union contracts protect these benefits.) There are programs to help people obtain or keep medical insurance, but not everyone is eligible for them. You can look into COBRA, which allows you to extend your health insurance through your job for 18 to 36 months. COBRA can be expensive as your employer no longer pays part of the premium. MassHealth may pay the premium. You can apply for health insurance directly from MassHealth, although workers comp benefits sometimes put injured workers just above the income limit. You can also apply at a hospital for free care. In addition, in 2006, health care reform legislation passed with the goal of providing some type of health insurance coverage to everyone in the state of Massachusetts. As this book goes to print, the details of these programs and the eligibility requirements are still being developed.

I lost my health insurance, and I didn't have any coverage for at least a year. I just did not go to the doctor. I hadn't gone to the dentist for a while. The chiropractor was helping me, so I was paying out-of-pocket for a number of years.

--------◆--------

I didn't have any health insurance for more than a year. I used homeopathic and over-the-counter remedies. For almost a year I went without my asthma medication. I didn't want to go to a doctor because I couldn't afford it. I was not eligible for MassHealth.

CHAPTER 14

CAN YOU TRUST YOUR DOCTOR?

I thought there was nothing wrong with going to the company doctor...I thought I had to stay with him...I thought it would be to my benefit to go. Then they would know I wasn't fudging.

After you reported your injury, your employer may have told you where to go for medical treatment. You may have assumed you had to go to that clinic or doctor. That is not the case. The law says that if your employer refers you to a preferred provider, you are required to see that physician *once*, and then you are free to go elsewhere.

What's wrong with the company doctor?

Perhaps the company doctor seems to be giving you the treatment you need, so you do not see a problem. In the early stages of your treatment, you are not thinking about building a legal case, and you are not sure what that would involve anyway. You expect to get better and go back to work soon.

Keep in mind that much of your case will hinge on medical evidence. This is frustrating because you know better than any doctor exactly what is happening to your body and what your limitations are. Usually, this information is contained in written reports rather than through actual testimony from the doctor.

Typically, preferred providers do provide some initial medical treatment, and they often will document injuries as work-related. They may be reluctant, however, to take you out of work or keep you out for as long as you need to heal. When you do have to go to court and present medical evidence, you may find that their reports are not written strongly in your favor.

This can have a negative effect on your case, but more importantly, these doctors can have *a negative effect on your health*. If you are pushed back to work before you are ready, you can injure yourself further. Now with a more severe injury, you may still not have the medical documentation to prove your case.

The sooner you get away from the company doctor the better, before there is a long paper trail that does not support your case. You do not want to be scrambling to find your own doctor right before you go before a judge. The judge may give more weight to the doctor who has been treating you for a long time.

What's wrong with a nurse case manager?

An insurer may try to assign a nurse case manager or medical manager to "assist" you with getting medical care. These nurse case managers can be very aggressive, sometimes going into the doctor's office with the patient. A few of them care about injured workers, but the majority of them know that their job is to serve the interest of the insurer. They may be writing reports for the insurer that say you are not in need of further medical treatment.

The nurse case manager may also come to your home, in order to "spy" and pass information on to a private investigator. You have the right to refuse the services of a nurse case manager. You do not need a nurse case manager to arrange medical treatment for you. You should be in charge of finding your own doctors and setting up your own appointments.

I had heard some negative remarks about our company doctor. One co-worker referred to him as Dr. Wait-and-See. But I had not been to a doctor for many years and still put them on a pedestal. Even after I started to mistrust him, I was afraid to go to another doctor. I thought a more independent, more competent doctor might tell me I had to go out of work or even that I would have to give up my profession. I was afraid of that. When the pain became unbearable, I finally asked if he would take me out of work for a while. He laughed, and joked that maybe he should send me to Hawaii, too. He asked me how long I thought he would last in his job if he did things like that. He had been saying all along that my condition was work-related, but in the end, he changed his mind, and wrote that he no longer thought work was the primary cause.

The Company Doctor Speaks

On April 10, 2003, a roundtable entitled "Managing an Injured Worker" was held at Mary Lane Hospital in Ware, Massachusetts. Dr. James R. Garb, director of Occupational Health & Safety for Baystate Health System, was the speaker. (Dr. Garb retired from this position in May 2006.) This was a rare opportunity to hear a preferred provider explain his views on injured workers. Most of the people attending were employers. We suspect that his patients would have been shocked by what he said.

Eighty percent of workers comp claims are legitimate, but 20 percent are "problem claims," complicated by "psychosocial factors," according to Dr. Garb. The handout he distributed said, "You pay disability for hurt feelings as well as for hurt backs." Employees may file claims because they feel powerless or face disciplinary action, he said. "This is their last shot to hold onto their job. It becomes one more thing for them to do in that limited repertoire they have." Psychosocial factors lead some workers to subconsciously delay their recovery, according to Dr. Garb.

"This is not the same as malingering. We see very little of that. But what we do see is this delayed recovery due to psychosocial factors. People are not even aware they're doing it. They're not crazy about their supervisor. They get more attention from their spouse."

At one point, Dr. Garb referred to his "clients." When asked if he was referring to his patients, Dr. Garb said he meant the employers. "We're sort of serving two masters in a way. We try to do what is right for the employee, but we also have an obligation to the company that is contracting with us."

Dr. Garb encouraged employers to call the physician about the injured worker. "We welcome your phone calls." It is very useful for the employer to tell the physician what the job entails (for example, lifting requirements). "It really does put the medical provider on your team. Otherwise, they're just relying on what the patient tells them."

He also encouraged employers to call the physician if the injured worker returns to work and then talks a great deal about a high likelihood of re-injury. "Call the provider and tell them what you're hearing so we are aware of it." This communication can occur without the patient knowing about it, Dr. Garb said. "It doesn't necessarily have to get back to the patient. If there's something you don't feel needs to be shared with the employee, we can talk about this." Dr. Garb also said the physician may call the employer to discuss suspicions about the patient. "I think that's certainly fair game for us to report back to the employer." The federal privacy law (HIPA) might require a release, Dr. Garb said.

Physicians are more willing to send an injured worker back to work if the employer is willing to make accommodations, but modified duty should not go on for too long, Dr. Garb said. "It can't just be a free ride to doing half your job." In dealing with "problem claims," he suggested that employers contact the injured workers regularly to ask how they are doing.

"You're sort of subtly making it clear that their convalescence is going to be monitored. You're creating a return to work expectation. You're letting them know you're sorry they're injured, but you expect them to come back." Spending more than two months out of work is a red flag for a potential "delayed recovery" case, he said. "There aren't many things that should keep you out that long."

Multiple diagnoses plus a history of depression or other psychiatric problems is a "big red flag." Injured workers may engage in "illness behavior," such as a patient's husband pushing her in a wheelchair. "They're trying to show you how much they're hurt."

Dr. Garb's handout listed other red flags: high absentee rates prior to the injury, reluctance to cooperate with treatment, inconsistent or non-organic physical findings, two or more weeks of hospitalization, disability out of proportion to the injury, cases which fail just before return to work, history of alcoholism or substance abuse, litigation pending, labor relations problems, and recent divorce or family crisis. In cases where the patient has seen more than one doctor and their opinions differ, Dr. Garb suggested an independent medical exam could be "an objective tie-breaker." (Independent medical examiners are doctors hired by the insurer.)

Dr. Garb maintained that employees are better off being treated by their employer's preferred provider rather than a physician of their own choosing. "The private physician's interest is in keeping the private patient happy, so if the patient says, 'Doc, I can't go back to work,' the doctor does not send them back to work." In contrast, Baystate's Occupational Health & Safety department operates on a "return-to-work" philosophy, he said. "It's best to get them back to work. It's therapeutic. Work is therapeutic for people who are injured."

CHAPTER 15

FINDING THE RIGHT DOCTOR

Research the doctors. Find out their histories. You've got to do your home-work.

Finding the right doctor is essential to your recovery. Also, the written evidence provided by the doctor will affect your ability to receive benefits, especially in the early stages before you are sent to an impartial medical examiner.

Who will pay the doctor?

Many injured workers mistakenly believe that they have to go to the company doctor because otherwise the insurer will not pay for medical treatment. The insurer is still required to pay for your medical treatment, even if you go to someone other than the company doctor.

You are entitled to reimbursement for mileage (30 cents per mile) and other travel costs, such as cab fares, tolls, and parking fees. You are also entitled to full payment for the cost of your prescription drugs. Save all of your receipts.

How much will the doctor charge?

The rates that doctors can charge are set by the DIA. A physician cannot charge you more or expect you to make up the difference between their charges and these rates. There are no co-payments. A different rate can be negotiated by the insurer, the employer and the health care provider (this happens sometimes in the case of surgery, not typically for office visits).

How do you find the right doctor?

If you have a positive relationship with your primary care doctor, you may want to start there. He or she may be able to refer you to a specialist. Talk to other injured workers about their experiences with doctors. You can also ask advocates, union representatives and lawyers. Research as much as you can the credentials of the physicians you are considering. You can get some basic information from the physician profiles on the website of the Massachusetts Board of Registration in Medicine (www.massmedboard.org).

How do you make the appointment?

Generally, you can call the office of the doctor you want to see and make an appointment. Be sure to tell the receptionist that the appointment is for a work injury, and provide the claim number. If you show up for an appointment without having first disclosed that the injury is work-related, the doctor may not see you. This is because treatment must be approved in advance by utilization review (more about this later).

If you still have an appointment with the company doctor, you can call and cancel it. You do not need permission from your employer or the insurer to make an appointment with another doctor.

Can a doctor refuse to take workers comp cases?

Physicians can refuse to take workers comp cases. Some consider the rates too low, and they do not want to be bothered with the paperwork and prior approvals. Some of the top physicians in their specialties do not take workers comp cases. The Alliance for Injured Workers has supported legislation that would raise the rates for doctors.

What types of problems arise with physicians?

Finding a physician on your own does not mean everything will go smoothly. Some physicians are most comfortable with established diagnoses that can be easily verified through x-rays or other test results. They may be skeptical of conditions such as multiple chemical sensitivity where the cause is not as easy to trace. Some doctors believe that if no objective finding can be found for a particular condition, it does not exist. Others will concede that there may be something wrong with you even if medical science has not yet found a way to measure it. Pain is subjective and invisible. Only you know to what extent you suffer from it.

Doctors' attitudes toward taking people out of work vary. Some are suspicious of injured workers. Others think it is good to keep patients working to avoid depression. The problem with such an approach is that continuing to work may worsen the injured worker's condition, delay recovery and eventually lead to a long period out of work. The result will be a much deeper depression.

If you cannot establish a good relationship with a particular physician, keep looking until you do find one with whom you feel comfortable. Sometimes this is regarded as "doctor shopping," or searching for a physician to support your case. In reality, injured workers are searching for doctors who believe them and acknowledge the true extent of their injuries. If you change doctors, the insurer is not required to pay for more than two doctors in the same specialty. The insurer may do so voluntarily or if ordered to by a DIA judge.

Request the records of your medical appointments. You need these to see what the doctor is writing about you. Some of our injured workers, who thought that they had a positive relationship with a particular doctor, have been surprised by what the doctor has written in medical records.

> *You've got to have your own records. So often, there is misinformation, including typos. It always happens. You're telling your doctor, he's speaking into a tape recorder and it's being transcribed somewhere else. The margin of error is so high.*

Who else will see your medical records?

The insurer will obtain copies of your medical records because it is paying for the treatment. Beware of signing any release that gives the insurer access to *all* of your medical records, even those unrelated to your work injury. Your lawyer will need to obtain your records and submit them as evidence supporting your case. The judge will read them, and they will eventually be given to the impartial medical examiner.

Sometimes, the insurer will try to use what is in your notes against you. Suppose you injured your back at work, but mention during a visit with your doctor that your back is worse that week because you lifted a heavy box at home. The insurer may jump on that information as proof that work is no longer the cause of your pain.

Medical Resources

MassHealth, the state's Medicaid program, provides health insurance to low-income individuals. Call 800-596-1276 for more information.

Health Care for All operates a Consumer Health Helpline. Call 800-272-4232 to find out if you qualify for MassHealth. www.hcfama.org.

Health Law Advocates is a nonprofit law firm that represents people in Massachusetts who are trying to gain access to health care. Services are restricted to people whose income does not exceed 300 percent of the federal poverty level. Health Law Advocates does not handle workers compensation or Social Security disability cases. The types of cases the firm does handle include denial of coverage by MassHealth or private insurance and denial of free care at hospitals. Health Law Advocates is associated with Health Care for All. The address is 30 Winter St. Ste. 1004, Boston, MA 02108; 617-338-5241. www.hla-inc.org.

Massachusetts has 52 *Community Health Centers* that offer a range of medical services to individuals regardless of their ability to pay (people with insurance can use these clinics also). Visit the web site of the Massachusetts League of Community Health Centers for more information: www.massleague.org.

CHAPTER 16

INDEPENDENT MEDICAL EXAMINERS

When I had to go to the doctor for the insurer, I felt treated like dirt. The doctor had zero bedside manner. I was being treated as if I did something wrong.

At some point, you may receive a letter in the mail notifying you that you must attend an independent medical exam. Often, this is a sign that the insurer is considering contesting your case. This is a doctor hired by the insurer to conduct a medical evaluation and write a report that may be used in court (probably against you).

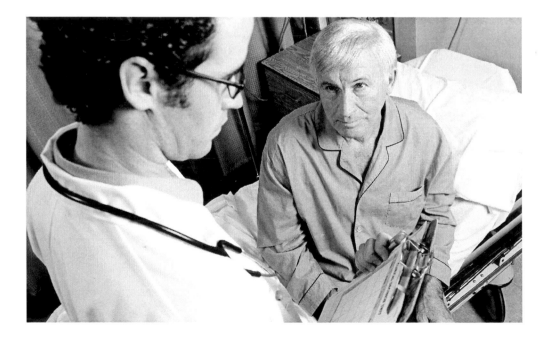

What will the independent medical examiner's report say?

Most of the time, these doctors write reports that favor the insurer. If an independent medical examiner repeatedly wrote medical reports that supported claims of injured workers, the insurer has the option of sending its business elsewhere. Occasionally, an insurer will send an injured worker to an independent medical examiner with a reputation for providing objective opinions because his or her reports will have greater credibility with a judge. In addition, if a report is not useful to the insurer, the insurer does not have to present it in court.

You probably will be upset when you read the independent medical examiner's report. It can be quite a shock to see how the facts are twisted by a doctor who has an agenda. The independent medical examiner can add to your emotional suffering. You are trying to recover, but you are caught in a system where your health problems are being contested, debated, and denied.

Do you have to attend an independent medical exam?

The insurer could cut off your benefits if you do not attend. The notice you receive in the mail may tell you to bring medical records and test results, such as x-rays, to the exam. You are not required to do this. After all, the exam is supposed to be "independent." While you have to attend an independent medical exam, you do not have to attend a functional capacity evaluation performed by a non-physician. This type of evaluation is ordered by the insurer to give the insurer "evidence" of what you are capable of doing.

What will happen during the exam?

The doctor will typically question you and then conduct a brief exam. He or she may ask questions about your activities outside of work or previous injuries in order to find another possible cause for your condition. These doctors sometimes use certain tests to try to determine if you are exaggerating your symptoms. One such test is to put their hands on top of your head and push down lightly, asking if this hurts. Supposedly, an affirmative answer indicates that you are a malingerer (an individual who is faking or exaggerating an injury).

How many times can the insurer send you to independent medical exams?

The law sets no limit on how many times the insurer can send you to an independent medical examiner. Individuals who have been awarded total and permanent disability benefits may be sent to independent medical examiners repeatedly. The insurer may take these reports to court to argue that the injured worker's condition has improved. This may be intended as a form of harassment designed to pressure the employee to settle.

How important are independent medical exams?

The good news about independent medical examiners is that most judges understand that they are not "independent" and do not give their opinions great weight. Much more important in the early stages are the reports from your own doctor. In the hearing stage of your case, the report from the impartial medical examiner is the most important piece of medical evidence.

CHAPTER 17

IMPARTIAL MEDICAL EXAMINERS

> *The most insane thing is the impartial medical examiner. His report was completely irrational. He stated all the facts, but his conclusion clearly did not follow from the facts... I was scared and angry of course, although I had heard how these things can be horrible. I felt helpless and I suppose a little bit depressed.*

Some time after your conference and before your hearing, you will receive a letter stating that you must attend an impartial medical exam. Although the language is similar, an impartial medical examiner is very different from the independent medical examiner described in the previous chapter. The impartial medical examiner's report will significantly affect the outcome of your case, for better or worse.

Why was the impartial medical exam created?

Prior to the 1991 "reform," judges reviewed medical reports from the injured worker's doctors and from independent medical examiners and came to a conclusion about the injured worker's condition. The number of reports slowed the process down. Also, since both sides chose their doctors, the objectivity of the reports was in question. The impartial physician report was created to make the system more efficient and fair. It has made the system more efficient. Because judges are required to use the report to determine the medical facts, they have an easier time deciding cases. Cases get heard more quickly than they did before 1991. We do not believe, however, that it has improved the fairness of the system. The system is supposed to be about justice, not efficiency. It gives too much power to one doctor. See Chapter 27 for a discussion of how the impartial system could be reformed.

After you go to an impartial physician exam, read the report carefully and discuss it with your lawyer. Does it say that you are totally or partially disabled (or not disabled at all)? Does it attribute your condition to work? Ask your physician about the chances of it being declared inadequate or whether a deposition would help.

Who can serve as an impartial physician?

An impartial physician must be fully licensed with the state, board certified, and have an active clinical practice. Some impartial physicians also serve as independent medical examiners for insurers. They are supposed to notify the DIA of any potential conflict. The DIA has difficulty finding a sufficient number of physicians interested in serving on their roster of impartial physicians. This can mean that you might have to travel to another part of the state. An impartial physician is paid $450 for a report.

It's outrageous, it's outrageous, especially when that person hasn't treated you and [is] looking through their own eyes, not through the eyes of the doctors who have cared for you being sick. It's a very intricate situation. There's too many things to look into to have someone look at you for just one day is crazy. I was sent to a specialist in hand surgery when I had spine surgery.

◆

I don't think it's fair because this impartial only sees you once and doesn't even take into consideration the doctor who the injured worker has established a relationship with and has seen more than once.

◆

I had strong reports from my doctors, linking my problems to work. I was certain that the impartial doctor's opinion couldn't be that much different from theirs. When I got a copy of my impartial's report, I was stunned.

CHAPTER 18

COMPLAINTS AGAINST DOCTORS

One doctor said, "Why don't you do something productive? Why don't you go back to work?" and another said, "You can't prove any of this."

Many of the injured workers who come to us for help have had bad experiences with doctors. Some formal complaint processes exist to deal with these types of complaints. Unfortunately, we have not seen injured workers have much success in pursuing complaints against physicians.

Can you sue for malpractice?

Suing for malpractice is not easy. First of all, you must find a lawyer who is interested in your case. A lawyer must spend thousands of dollars to prepare such a case. Therefore, few lawyers want to accept a case where the expected damages would be less than the expenses. You may have been the victim of negligence and suffered as a result, but you may be unable to find a lawyer willing to represent you. If you do

find a lawyer to represent you, there are still more hurdles. According to Massachusetts General Laws (Ch. 231, Sec. 60B), your case must first be addressed to a tribunal consisting of a justice of the Superior Court, a physician and a lawyer. The tribunal decides whether or not there is enough evidence for your case to proceed further. You have three years after the incident (or three years after you became aware of the negligence) to sue. The time between the incident and your filing a lawsuit cannot exceed seven years (M.G.L. Ch. 260, Sec. 4). You cannot sue an independent or impartial medical examiner for medical malpractice because there is no doctor-patient relationship.

The drawback to pursuing a lawsuit is that it may consume your time and emotional energy for years with no guarantee of satisfaction in the end. In addition, a medical malpractice lawsuit for treatment of a work-related injury or illness is considered a third party claim. See Chapter 20 for an explanation of third-party lawsuits.

Are there other avenues for complaints?

You can file a complaint about a physician with the Massachusetts Board of Registration in Medicine, 560 Harrison Avenue, Suite G-4, Boston, MA 02118, www.massmedboard.org. Just as it may be very frustrating to pursue a lawsuit, it may be frustrating to seek vindication through the Board of Registration in Medicine. The board may take a long time to respond, and in the end, dismiss your complaint, leaving you feeling angry and invalidated. They are most likely to take action in cases where the doctor violated a rule or was obviously negligent. More subtle complaints, such as the quality of your care, are less likely to result in action.

Peruse the press releases on the board's website concerning past disciplinary actions. This will give you some idea of what types of behavior lead to action. It may be worthwhile to make a complaint even if it does not result in any action. The complaint letter will stay in the physician's file and may be useful if someone makes a similar complaint.

> *I made a complaint to the medical board about the company doctor. I thought he had made my condition worse by giving me such poor treatment. I did not hear anything for several months. When I finally called to check, the woman asked me, "Is this a workers comp case? Oh, we get those all the time. We never do anything with them." I never even received an official letter telling me that my complaint had been dismissed.*

If your physician works at a hospital, you can complain to the hospital or to the Joint Commission on Accreditation of Healthcare Organizations, the organization that accredits most hospitals. The address is Office of Quality Monitoring, JCAHO, One Renaissance Boulevard, Oakbrook Terrace, IL 60181. The web address is, www.jointcommission.org. In addition, the DIA's Health Care Services Board investigates complaints against health care practitioners providing services to injured workers. The Health Care Services Board investigates complaints of discrimination against workers comp claimants, overutilization of procedures (such as unnecessary surgery), and other inappropriate treatment. Their address is the DIA, Health Care Services Board, 600 Washington Street, 7th Floor, Boston, MA 02111. The website is www.mass.gov/dia.

CHAPTER 19

LAWYERS: WHO NEEDS THEM?

I have never had to call a lawyer before, and I thought of myself as a person who would never need to call a lawyer. I'm a good person. I didn't think I'd need to call a lawyer.

You are not required to hire a lawyer, but we recommend that you do. In fact, it is probably a good idea to find a lawyer in the early stages *before* the insurer begins to hassle you. Many injured workers are reluctant to hire a lawyer. Some are worried about the fee. Others worry that getting a lawyer is an adversarial step against their employer.

What will a lawyer cost?

You will not be charged for an initial consultation. You can decide after that if you want to proceed further. The fees for lawyers who handle workers comp cases are set by law. They are paid by the insurer if you win in court. The lawyer does not charge you, and does not get paid, if you lose. If you settle your case, however, your lawyer can take no more than 20 percent of a settlement in an accepted case and no more than 15 percent in an unaccepted case. There may be times when you will be expected to pay for some expenses or the fee for an appeal. Be sure to discuss all of this with your lawyer so there are no surprises.

If you prevail at your conference, and the judge orders the insurer to pay you benefits, the insurer must pay your lawyer a fee set by the DIA. (The fee varies based on the nature of the dispute and the outcome.) If you prevail at your hearing, the insurer must pay your lawyer $5,233.64 plus necessary expenses. If you lose at the conference or hearing, your lawyer is paid nothing. These were the fees as of October 1, 2008. The system provides an incentive for lawyers to work hard on behalf of their clients, and it opens the door to the courtroom for injured workers who cannot afford to pay a lawyer.

The fee arrangement is different for appeals to the Reviewing Board. If the insurer appeals a hearing decision to the Reviewing Board and loses, then the insurer must pay your lawyer $1,495.34. If *you* appeal to the Reviewing Board, you are responsible for paying a fee agreed upon between you and your lawyer. Again, be sure to discuss the fee arrangement in advance.

Why do you need a lawyer?

In addition to concern over fees, many injured workers worry that hiring a lawyer will anger their employer. They do not want to "fight" with their employer; they just want to get the medical care or benefits they need. This is the "roll over and play dead" approach. If you have this attitude, you are assuming that the less assertive you are about your rights, the nicer the insurer and your employer will be to you. Sometimes, decisions about your case are out of your employer's hands. The decisions are made far away in the office of an insurance company. Therefore, the fact that you have had a good relationship with your employer does not mean you will be treated well.

Neither your employer nor the insurer will explain your rights to you. Hiring a lawyer does not mean you are going to "war." It does not mean you are going to sue your employer. (Workers comp insurance protects your employer from lawsuits.) It means that you will have someone knowledgeable about the system on your side. Your lawyer will notify the insurer that you are being represented, but will not need to take any action unless you are denied benefits. The insurer will no longer be able to contact you directly.

Some injured workers doubt that their case is serious enough to require the services of a lawyer. They are unsure if any lawyer would be interested. Incredibly, we have heard this concern from people with serious injuries that have kept them out of work for a long time and who are already having trouble with the insurer. Most lawyers are willing to take on cases even in the early stages when the insurer is still treating you well. They can prepare you for what is to come. They would rather you come to them early before you make mistakes that could make it difficult to win your case. They want to sign you up for their services before another lawyer does. Some have lists of physicians in the area. It is unlikely that a lawyer will think your case is too trivial.

I thought you needed a lawyer when you weren't really hurt. I thought that was a sign you were trying to get something for nothing.

◆

I didn't think I had to get a lawyer. I didn't think I had to defend myself.

◆

He did an awesome job for me. I don't think lawyers are particularly compassionate people. That's probably not their job, but when you're dealing with injured people who are going through a lot of serious pain and trau-

ma...I don't know, it would just help if they took a 101 in compassion. They may be immune to it. They see it day in and day out. He was extremely knowledgeable, but just seemed to lack compassion.

----◆----

To the lawyers, it's a day of work. It's not their life. Don't ever think they're thinking about it the same way as you are.

----◆----

I picked my lawyer out of the phone book. He impressed me when I met him. Yet, when I finally went to court, a different lawyer from the same firm showed up. He asked me what my injury was.

----◆----

I did feel confident that my lawyer did have my best interest at heart. I felt that my lawyer did hear what I was going through and was empathetic and really did support me.

----◆----

Pretty much, in general, I found compassion depends upon personality. In general, I would say yes, my lawyer was compassionate.

How do you find the right lawyer?

While we think it is important to find a lawyer early, we must caution you to be careful about the lawyer that you choose. You may find it difficult to switch lawyers later if you are dissatisfied. Most lawyers will not want to meet with you if you are already represented.

Therefore, you may be in a position where you have to fire your lawyer before you can search for another one. This can be scary if you are in the middle of adjudicating your case at the DIA. Even after you make a formal break with your first lawyer, you may find that some lawyers do not want to take on a case that another lawyer has already handled. If you complain about your first lawyer, other lawyers may view you as difficult, and be wary of representing you.

Therefore, do not choose your lawyer from the phone book. Do not go to a lawyer just because he or she is a friend or relative. The lawyer who wrote your will or handled a real estate transaction for you is not necessarily the best lawyer to handle your workers comp case. These individuals may genuinely want to help you, but you are better off finding a lawyer who handles workers comp cases all the time. Talk to other injured workers and find out what their experiences have been.

Some workers comp lawyers only represent injured workers, while others work both sides of the fence, representing both injured workers and employers. You may feel more comfortable with lawyers who represent only injured workers. On the other hand, lawyers who work both sides may have valuable experience that will help them represent you.

What are some common complaints about lawyers?

Even when you have been careful with the lawyer you select, problems may arise. A lawyer who gave you a lot of time and attention during the initial consultation may be hard to reach later. Not returning phone calls promptly is a common complaint about lawyers. Even after a lump sum settlement has been reached, your lawyer should still be available to help if you have issues with the insurer, such as unpaid prescriptions or mileage.

Many injured workers have had positive experiences with their lawyers, but others have reported that their lawyers were abrasive and insensitive. For the injured worker who is scared, depressed and desperate, the relationship with a lawyer can be another source of stress.

Lawyers often are no help in dealing with the severe emotional distress you are experiencing. The time they spend talking to you on the phone will be limited. They are skilled at explaining what the law says, not at providing emotional support or finding creative solutions to the myriad of problems that you are facing.

Although your lawyer knows much more about the law and the system than you do, non-disabled people never truly understand disability. An excellent workers comp lawyer may not be knowledgeable about other programs, such as food stamps or Section 8, that might help you. If you are unsuccessful in obtaining workers comp benefits, your lawyer may have little to offer in terms of what you should do next.

If you are permanently disabled, your life will change dramatically. You will have to get help in addition to your lawyer. Other disabled people are the best source of survival skills. Network with other people who are more knowledgeable about the system.

If your relationship with your lawyer deteriorates to the point where you are considering hiring another lawyer, call your lawyer first and ask to meet to resolve the problems. Always listen to the advice of your lawyer, but remember that you are in charge and have the right to make the final decisions.

Legal Resources

Massachusetts Commission Against Discrimination

One Ashburton Place, Sixth Floor, Room 601

Boston, MA 02108

617-994-6000; www.mass.gov/mcad

Springfield Office: 436 Dwight St.,

Second Floor, Room 220, Springfield, MA 01103

413-739-2145

Disability Law Center

11 Beacon St., Suite 925, Boston, MA 02108

617-723-8455; www.dlc-ma.org

Office of Attorney General
Division of Fair Labor

(Enforces employment law)

Boston: 617-727-3465

Springfield: 413-784-1128

Worcester: 508-792-7600

New Bedford: 508-990-9700

www.ago.state.ma.us

CHAPTER 20

THIRD-PARTY LAWSUITS

"It's not all it's cracked up to be. It was a joke."

You cannot sue your employer for a work injury unless your employer lacks workers comp insurance. Co-workers cannot be sued because they have the same protection as the employer. You may be able to sue a third party, however. This is someone other than your employer or co-workers who is responsible for or contributed to your injuries.

What is a third-party lawsuit?

In a third-party lawsuit, you can get compensation for medical bills, lost wages and pain and suffering. The catch is that if you win or settle your third-party lawsuit, the workers comp insurer is entitled to be reimbursed for their claim payments. They cannot get more money from you than you recover from the third party.

Who can you sue?

- The manufacturer, distributor or seller of the machine, chemicals or product that injured you
- The property owner if your employer does not own the property where you were hurt
- The general contractor of a project you are working on or another subcontractor working on the same project
- The driver of another vehicle in a motor vehicle accident that happens on the job

How long do you have to file?

Depending on the location and circumstances of your injury, you may have up to three years to file after your injury or illness occurs. The time limit could be less than three years, so speak to a lawyer as soon as possible after the injury. You will need to find an experienced personal injury lawyer.

CHAPTER 21

GOING BACK TO WORK

I'm still in denial that I've left my job. When I left that day, I didn't think it was going to be my last day there. I really thought I was going to go back in some way, shape or form.

You may recover from your injury, return to your previous work, and resume a normal life. If your injury is severe enough, you may never work again. Or, you may find yourself somewhere between these two extremes. Perhaps you think you might be able to do a different type of work or part-time work. Once you are injured, you are faced with many questions and decisions regarding work. Should you continue to try to work in pain? Does your employer have to offer light duty? Can your employer fire you while you are out of work? Some injured workers continue to work in pain for as long as they can after being injured. Those that go out of work want to return quickly, but that is not always possible. We all know that being out of work is not a vacation; it's a nightmare.

Should you work while injured?

You may be continuing to work despite your injury. You are entitled to payment of your medical bills. Ask yourself if continuing to work is the best option. If you are able to perform the job without additional pain and further injury, then this is a perfectly reasonable choice. If you are continuing to work because you are afraid of the consequences of going out on workers comp, consider whether you are making the best choice for your health. Further injuring yourself will only make your case more complicated and could delay or prevent a full recovery.

If some of your work tasks are causing pain, is there special equipment or some other accommodation that could help? You can request these from your employer. Your employer's obligation to provide them is not always clear. The Americans with Disabilities Act requires your employer to make "reasonable" accommodations, but what qualifies as reasonable is a gray area in the law.

Should you go back to work?

If you have been out of work for a while, you may be unsure if you are ready to go back. Your doctor may send you back with certain restrictions. If you resume working, but have to go out again within 28 days, you do not need to file another claim in order to get benefits from the insurer. Generally, it is a good idea to try to decide if you can continue before the 28 days end, but continuing to work beyond this period does not make you ineligible for benefits.

What is light duty?

Light duty means a change in working conditions that enables you to work despite your limitations. If your injury makes it difficult to stand, for example, a desk job would be light duty. What is "light duty" varies from person to person. The general public might regard ditch digging as heavy labor and office work as light duty. Yet, people with spinal injuries often have difficulty sitting for long periods and find deskwork painful. Many office jobs now involve use of the computer, and these jobs are not light duty for individuals with repetitive strain injuries.

Does your employer have to offer light duty?

Your employer is not obligated to provide light duty. Some employers will provide it, at least for a while, because it is to their benefit to have you doing some work. If you are interested in requesting light duty, have your doctor put the restrictions you need in writing.

Do you have to accept an offer of light duty?

Sometimes, the initiative comes from the employer. If the employer makes you an offer of light duty that follows the written restrictions set out by your doctor, and you refuse that offer, your case could be adversely affected. You can try to argue that the offer would create a hardship. Suppose, for example, your employer said that light duty was only available on the overnight shift. A judge would decide whether it is a hardship or an inconvenience.

If you attempt light duty and find you are unable to do it, explain this to your doctor and see if he or she is willing to alter the restrictions or write that you need to be out of work.

If you have a written offer from your employer that matches a written statement from your doctor about the type of duties you can perform, that will be considered evidence of your earning capacity and could be used to reduce your benefits. Actual earnings will also be used to determine earning capacity. Sometimes, injured workers who diligently continue working in pain hurt their own chances of getting workers comp. The fact that you are working will be used as evidence that you *can* work, regardless of how painful it is.

Can your employer fire you?

The law offers little protection from being fired while you are out on workers comp. Your employer cannot fire you as retaliation for filing a claim, but can let you go if you are unable to return to work. In a small business with only a handful of employees, an employer could argue that the business cannot function with your position vacant. If you suspect the real motive is retaliation, the burden will be on you to prove it. If you are fortunate enough to belong to a union, your contract may provide some protection against being fired and may also require the employer to provide light duty. Once you have been terminated, you have a right to preference in rehiring "provided, however, that a suitable job is available" (M.G.L. Ch. 152, Sec. 75A).

The Family and Medical Leave Act may protect your job for up to 12 weeks. You can file for time off under the FMLA at the same time that you are pursuing a workers comp claim and collecting benefits. You must have worked 12 months or 1,250 hours for a company with at least 50 full-time employees.

Your employer may come to you, insisting that you apply for FMLA. Employers do this because they know that their obligation will end after

12 weeks. If you request FMLA later in the year for the same or a different reason, some or all of your 12 weeks will already be used. You do not have a right to refuse to use FMLA if your employer wants you to apply. For more information, contact the U.S. Dept. of Labor, Wage and Hour Bureau, JFK Federal Building, Boston, MA 02203, (617) 624-6700.

Who can force you back to work?

You may feel as if the doctors, your employer and the insurer are much more powerful than you are. The language we use often implies this. You may say, "The doctor sent me back to work," or, "My company ordered me back to work." You may receive an intimidating letter from your company "ordering" you back to work by a certain date. Your lawyer, thinking strictly of what is good for your case, may advise you to follow "doctor's orders" and go back to work with restrictions when you do not feel you can.

Some injured workers hear that the insurer is *denying* their claim and think that means they *must* return to work. They do not even realize that they have a right to fight the insurer through the DIA. Some injured workers think that an independent medical examiner has the power to send them back to work. That is not so. Other injured workers tell us, "The company doctor keeps sending me back to work," not realizing that they have a right to find their own doctor (who might be less interested in serving the company's interests).

It is important to remember that no one can *force* you to work. Not your employer, not the insurer, not your doctor, or even a judge. A judge decides whether or not you are entitled to benefits while out of work, but cannot make you return. Obviously, there can be serious consequences if you do not work when your treating doctor says you can, and you may not feel as if you have much of a choice. Give careful thought to what is best for your body, your workers comp case and your immediate and long-term financial well being.

What if you disagree with your doctor's assessment of your ability to work? You are truly injured, but your doctor is not willing to write that you need to be out of work. This can happen for any number of reasons. Some doctors are afraid patients are trying to get a "vacation." The doctor cannot measure your pain, and there may not be "objective" test results (MRI, X-rays, etc.) to corroborate the severity of your injury. This does not mean you are not truly injured; just that medical science has no way of measuring it.

You certainly have the option of looking for another doctor. This may be viewed by the system as "doctor shopping," i.e., looking for a doctor who says what you want. It may be necessary for your health, however, to find a doctor who understands how bad your condition is.

Ideally, you and your doctor are on the same page, but this does not always happen. This can be one of the most difficult and frightening situations for an injured worker. If your doctor says you are ready to go back to work, and you are not ready, you do have the option of not returning. You will have great difficulty obtaining workers comp benefits, and you open the door wide for your company to fire you.

Still, in some situations, it may be the right decision. Some of us in the Alliance for Injured Workers have permanent injuries, causing constant pain, which could have been avoided had we not gone back to work repeatedly to injure ourselves further. Your immediate focus is probably on the short-term. You want to keep your job and win your case. Losing your job or your workers comp benefits seems like a disaster, and they probably are. Yet, having a curable condition turn into an incurable condition is also a disaster that will have *lifelong* implications. You will have to weigh all of these factors before making a decision.

If you have a condition such as repetitive strain injury that began as a mild condition and has gradually worsened, beware of the possibility that you could have permanent problems with your hands, arms and neck. If you have been stuck in a cycle of going out of work, feeling better, returning to work and then feeling worse, assess realistically whether or not you can continue working in a repetitive job. Perhaps you can plan for a new career before your injury becomes so disabling that even retraining is difficult or impossible.

WORK AND SOCIAL SECURITY DISABILITY BENEFITS

Some injured workers with severe, debilitating injuries apply for Social Security disability benefits. These are difficult to obtain. See Chapter 24 for more information. If you do obtain them, the good news is that you can often attempt to work without jeopardizing your disability income. There are two programs for disabled individuals, SSI and SSDI. Many injured workers, because of their work history, will qualify for SSDI. Make sure you know which type of benefits you are receiving because the rules are very different for each. It is generally not a good idea to attempt to work (even part time) while you are trying to obtain these benefits. Of course, this is a Catch-22, because you may wait more than a year to get accepted for Social Security.

Once you are approved, your benefits should continue as long as you are earning less than what is considered substantial and gainful employment. In 2008, this figure was $940 per month. There are many incentives and "trial-work periods" to help disabled individuals attempt to return to work without fear of losing their benefits if these attempts are unsuccessful.

Because the work rules are so complicated, we cannot explain them thoroughly here. We can only provide an overview. Since it is so important that you do not jeopardize your benefits, we would recommend you consult with a benefits specialist (described below) before attempting work. The Social Security Administration has pamphlets that explain the rules. In addition, a program called BenePLAN, run by the Resource Partnership, helps residents of Berkshire, Franklin, Hampden and Hampshire counties understand the work rules. Call 888-421-8919, ext. 120. If you live in Middlesex or Worcester counties, call 877 YES WORK, ext. 14. In other areas of the state, call the Impact program, run by the Massachusetts Rehabilitation Commission, at 800-734-7475.

CHAPTER 22

RETRAINING

I think I would restructure the workplace and the jobs themselves. They could reconstruct some new jobs. Working at home...I could have done charts at home. I have my computer.

You may reach a point where you are unable to return to your previous job and are unable to earn your previous wages. There are programs that can help you retrain if that is appropriate. They include the DIA's Office of Education and Vocational Rehabilitation and the Massachusetts Rehabilitation Commission. You can request help from both agencies.

Does vocational rehabilitation include retraining?

The DIA Office of Education and Vocational Rehabilitation (OEVR) is supposed to help you return to work, but retraining you for another job is a last resort. Unfortunately, the goal of the DIA is to *restore* your earning capacity, not *enhance* it. Therefore, if you were working as a waitress, the DIA will not approve a plan to send you to medical school. First, a counselor (paid for by the insurer) evaluates whether you can return to the same job with modifications or to a different job with the same employer. If not, a counselor may offer vocational testing and help you search for a job with another employer. If these options are ruled out, you may be a candidate for retraining.

Can you refuse these services?

The insurer can initiate the process, and then you will receive a letter telling you to attend a mandatory meeting. If you refuse to go, your benefits could be suspended. "The employee's right to compensation shall also be suspended during any period the employee refuses the insurer's written request that the employee be evaluated by a vocational rehabilitation specialist for the DIA" (M.G.L. Ch. 152, Sec. 45). The office will review your medical status, job skills, history and education to determine eligibility. The office can decide that you are eligible even if you do not feel ready. You do not have to cooperate, but your benefits may be cut by 15 percent.

Who pays for the services?

Often, it is the insurer who pays for vocational rehabilitation. If the DIA develops a rehabilitation plan for you, and the insurer refuses to pay for it, the DIA can pay for the training out of a special trust fund. If you successfully complete the program and return to suitable employment, the DIA can assess the insurer twice the cost incurred. The money will be put back in the trust fund.

Does settling your case make you ineligible?

If you settle, and are entitled to vocational rehabilitation, you will have two years to request these services. If you have been deemed suitable for vocational rehabilitation and have not yet completed a rehabilitation program, you cannot enter a lump sum agreement without approval from the OEVR.

What other help is available besides the DIA?

The Massachusetts Rehabilitation Commission may also be able to help you return to work. In fact, you may find the Massachusetts Rehabilitation Commission to be more helpful than the DIA. The commission sometimes pays for classes as well as adaptive equipment. The commission may be able to help you even if you are only able to perform part-time work.

CHAPTER 23

PREJUDICE AGAINST PEOPLE WITH DISABILITIES

My own mother was making the assumption that I was milking the system because I wanted to stay home and eat bon-bons and watch the home-shopping channel. She didn't believe that I was really in pain and was injured. It's an invisible injury. If I had a neck brace on; if I was walking around with crutches or a cast or had to go and have surgery and had stitches, then that's acceptable.

Your period of disability may last a few weeks, a few months, or a lifetime. If it is short-term, you will need some help getting through a tough period. If it is chronic, you will need to change the way you live.

Many injured workers do not realize that they have a permanent disability until *years* after they are injured. They think that they are going back to work. They go through numerous traditional and alternative medical treatments, hoping something will cure them. Eventually, they learn strategies for surviving psychologically and financially.

When this happens it changes everything about you. It isn't just the injury, it's a life change.

One of the challenges people with disabilities face is prejudice. In a society that measures people by their professional achievements and financial success, the individual who does not work is regarded with disdain. This is especially ironic given how hard many injured workers try to keep working. The contempt and demeaning comments can be as painful as the disability.

What are the roots of this prejudice?

People whose bodies have never failed them really do not understand disability. They have probably worked while sick and deep down they wonder why you cannot. Our culture praises and admires the athlete or individual who accomplishes something despite pain.

Several years ago, a speaker at one of our meetings offered advice on how to hold onto assets, such as a house. He began by saying, "Some of you may have to make some tough choices. You may have to go back to work."

When we were interviewing to hire an advocate for injured workers, one candidate said that he would challenge anyone who claimed an inability to work. The problem, he said, was probably psychological with the person just being too depressed to get out of bed. Clearly, these individuals did not understand that some injured workers do not have a choice. They are not able to work.

How will co-workers react?

Workers should help and support other workers who become injured. After all, they may find themselves in the same situation. Unfortunately, co-workers are not always supportive. They may resent the fact that they have to work while you do not. In an understaffed workplace, workers may feel burdened when another employee is out. Co-workers may understand little about your financial and emotional stress. They do not realize how lucky they are not to be injured. If they see you out and about, they may question whether your injury is real. One injured worker with a severe back injury requested a special chair from her employer. When it arrived, another employee snidely remarked, "What do I have to do to get one of those?"

> *I said I was going to leave to go to the doctor. The other two nurses got upset that I was leaving...I heard later that they said, "She didn't want to be here anyway."*

----◆----

> *A woman I worked with told me that her grandmother had worked for years on a typewriter with no problems, so she didn't understand what the problem was with working on a computer.*

Will family members be supportive?

Families can be and often are a great source of support when a worker is injured. But disability of one partner can put great stress on a marriage. Many couples depend on two incomes and have little in reserves when one of them becomes disabled. Resentment builds up when one partner goes to work and the other stays home. Your husband or wife may not understand why you cannot work.

Do professionals share these prejudices?

You may encounter prejudice from people who are supposed to be helping you. We have had several vocational rehabilitation counselors as guests at our meetings. One pointed out that the first question people ask when meeting is, "What do you do?" If you have no answer, you are likely to feel embarrassed, he said, adding that was a good reason to retrain and go back to work. Another vocational expert told us that the alternative to retraining is "sitting on the couch." What these "experts" did not realize is that not everyone can retrain and resume working full time. There will always be a percentage who cannot work at all. This is not due to a lack of motivation. Many of them are in chronic pain and struggling to perform tasks of daily living.

You may decide at some point to seek psychological counseling. There are a wide range of approaches, philosophies and techniques. A therapist who focuses on childhood may have little to offer with regard to your present struggles. Be on guard against therapists who want to attribute your physical problems to psychological causes, as well as those who mistake your desire to avoid pain for a lack of motivation.

How can the disability rights movement help?

Injured workers have much to learn by connecting with other groups of disabled people who are much more experienced in advocating for their rights. Just learning to think of yourself as part of an oppressed group puts your struggles in a different light. The disabled are a diverse group, however. Some segments are underemployed because their abilities have been underestimated. The emphasis on their capabilities has left the public with the misleading impression that anyone with a disability can work with the right accommodations. People with invisible injuries complain that no one recognizes their limitations. When they need help, they do not get it. They do not want pity, but they would prefer some compassion to the hostility they often encounter.

A friend of mine knew I was getting both workers comp and SSDI, but I was a candidate for that. She said, "Who's paying for this? Are we, the taxpayers?" I was so horrified. I will never forget it. It was just the most horrible thing someone could have said to me. I paid into the system. I paid my dues, and those things are put in place for us to take advantage of when we are injured. The attitude toward us, it is like we are lepers.

◆

When my daughter was young she belonged to a Brownie troop and the mom was on disability. I used to remember seeing her conduct the meetings and see her interact with the girls, and I used to think, "Gee, she looks like she's doing fine." She talked one day about what it took to do Brownies. Initially I was skeptical. But then I saw her on those days. It helped me change my perspective or idea. It was an eye-opener.

◆

Even people at church, they were very understanding, but I was ashamed to even talk to them or people that I met. They said, "What do you do?" I had a double whammy to say, "No, I'm injured, and my employer laid me off."

◆

I had a therapist once who told me, "You're not sick." And I thought, "If you could just be in my place." She said, "You're not sick. You could go get a job."

CHAPTER 24

FINANCIAL SURVIVAL

Lifestyling down was a lot harder than lifestyling up.

Sharing survival strategies is one of the ways we help each other at the Alliance for Injured Workers. Since you have worked for a number of years, you are probably unfamiliar with the programs designed to help low-income people. Maybe you have assumed you will get better and return to work, so you have not bothered to investigate or apply for these programs. Or, perhaps you have assumed that your home or savings make you ineligible. This chapter lists some resources for surviving financially.

What are possible sources of income?

Social Security

Social Security has two programs that help the disabled: Social Security Disability Insurance (SSDI) and Supplemental Security Income (SSI). To apply, call the Social Security Administration at 800-772-1213. Injured workers with permanent, disabling injuries often end up applying for SSDI. Injured workers who "lose" their workers comp cases also are often forced to turn to Social Security to survive.

Who is eligible for SSDI? You must have paid enough Social Security tax to have earned a sufficient number of "credits." The number of "credits" needed to qualify varies with age. The Social Security Administration's website, www.ssa.gov, has a detailed explanation of how these credits are earned. Teachers and other state and municipal workers with a separate retirement plan may not be eligible. Generally, if you have been working steadily for a number of years in a private sector job and contributing to Social Security, you will meet the requirements for SSDI. If you wait a long time to apply, you may lose money since Social Security will only pay retroactive benefits for up to one year prior to the date you apply. SSDI benefits are not payable for the first five months a claimant is disabled.

You must be totally, permanently disabled, but that is defined as an inability to perform substantial, gainful employment for at least one year. In 2009, substantial, gainful employment was $980 or more per month of gross earnings. This amount is increased each year to adjust for inflation. You do not have to be out of work for a year before applying.

You must have a doctor willing to say that your period of disability will last at least a year.

It is sometimes possible to collect SSDI *in addition* to workers comp benefits, though there may be an offset. Social Security will not allow your workers comp check and SSDI to add up to more than 80 percent of your previous work income. A lump sum settlement in your workers comp case does not necessarily have to affect your future SSDI payments. Your lawyer may be able to structure the settlement to avoid or minimize this. See Chapter 10 for more information.

Injured workers who have permanent, severe disabilities often survive on SSDI after settling their workers comp cases. Many injured workers find it easier to live under the Social Security system than under the highly adversarial workers comp system. Once you have been accepted, there are provisions in the system that allow you to work part-time, and even attempt full-time work without fear of losing your benefits. See Chapter 21.

Although SSDI may be very helpful once you have been approved, getting approved is not easy. After fighting your way through the workers comp system, you may be very discouraged to have to take on another fight. It is not uncommon to be rejected twice and then wait months for a hearing before a judge.

Getting on SSDI could take a year or longer. Many workers comp lawyers also handle Social Security disability claims, but you do not have to use the same lawyer. There are lawyers whose practices are devoted largely to Social Security disability. If you get approved for SSDI, your lawyer will take 25 percent of your retroactive benefits or $5,300, which-ever is less. If you are not approved, you will not have to pay the lawyer.

Talk to others who have applied. There is a lot of knowledge amongst people who have been through this process. Getting accepted will be difficult, and you may be tempted to give up. Many people whose cases seemed hopeless eventually were approved.

Here are some tips:

- If possible, do not work *while trying to get on* SSDI, even if the pay you earn is less than substantial, gainful employment. This seems to have a negative effect on an applicant's chances.

- Once accepted, do not work right up to the limit of substantial, gainful employment. That will make it easy for Social Security to say you could earn just a little more.

- If you cite depression and anxiety as reasons you cannot work, Social Security will not give much weight to these claims unless you produce evidence of treatment, such as seeing a psychiatrist or therapist and taking medication.

- Not taking medication to treat emotional problems could hurt your chances of getting SSDI. Of course, the choice is yours. You may not want to take medication for a variety of valid reasons. Just be aware that Social Security may view this as an unwillingness to treat a disabling condition.

- Certain professionals are not considered qualified to speak to your residual functional capacity (what you can still do despite the mental or physical impairments you have). The opinion of a psychiatrist or clinical psychologist would be considered, while the opinion of a counselor with a master's degree in social work could be considered, but is likely to be given much less weight. If your treatment for depression consists of counseling with a social worker, Social Security may send you to a psychiatrist of their choosing for an evaluation.

• Once accepted, how often you are reviewed can vary, but a common interval is every three years. One factor they look for is continued medical treatment. If you have not seen a doctor in a long time, that will raise suspicion.

SSI (Supplemental Security Income) also provides benefits to the disabled. The program was designed primarily for individuals who do not have a long enough work history to be eligible for SSDI. If your SSDI benefit falls below a minimum, Social Security may supplement it with SSI. The differences between these programs are dramatic. SSDI is a much better program. Your house, your savings, and other assets accumulated while you worked will not affect your eligibility for SSDI. Having more than $2,000 in countable assets will disqualify you for SSI. The work rules are not as generous on SSI.

> *[Applying for SSDI] The word failure comes to mind. Embarrassed. A supposed friend said, "If you can do this and you can do that, why can't you work 40 hours a week?" She didn't realize that I would rest in order to do something. If I went to a family gathering, I would stay overnight because I could not drive back that same day. It took twice as long to do anything as before.*

---- ◆ ----

> *At one point, I went for more than a year with no income at all! I had savings, but I worried all the time about losing everything I had. I kept asking for help and doors kept slamming in my face. I could not seem to make people understand that I could not work. I was denied Social Security disability repeatedly. When I finally got it, I was thrilled even though it was less than $11,000 a year.*

Private disability insurance

Your health is your most valuable asset. Without it, your ability to make money is severely limited. Most people insure their vehicles and their homes, but few insure their bodies against disability. Perhaps the idea of becoming disabled is so frightening that many people do not want to think about it. Once you are disabled, you will not be able to obtain this type of coverage.

A private disability policy may give you income in addition to workers comp or Social Security. This can be very valuable, providing you with an income close to the one you had while working. Still, insurance companies rarely part with their money easily. The insurer may contest your claim, send you to independent medical examiners, and have you followed.

How can you keep a roof over your head?

There are several housing programs that may help you. The Section 8 Housing Choice Voucher Program was created to give low-income people a choice where they want to live, rather than being concentrated in urban housing "projects." The government pays a percentage of your rent. The criteria for eligibility are complicated and include certain "priority" categories. Unfortunately, the waiting list for this program is years. We recommend that you apply anyway since you never know what your situation will be in several years.

You can also apply to a local housing authority to live in housing for the elderly and disabled. You do not have to apply only to the complex in your own community. The wait to get accepted is usually months, not years. (This is true unless you have children. The wait for the small number of family units could be years.) The apartments are small, but all of the utilities (except phone) are generally included in the rent, which is a percentage of your income. Many times, all the housing authorities require is a letter from a physician stating that you have a medical condition expected to be of long duration. You do not have to go through a long, adversarial process to prove that you are disabled.

A program called Residential Assistance for Families in Transition (RAFT) is designed to help families that are homeless or at risk of becoming homeless. (It is not available to single people.) Your total income must be at or below 50 percent of the median income in your area.

How will you get food to eat?

Contact your local office of Transitional Assistance to find out if you are eligible for food stamps. Although this program considers assets when determining eligibility, some assets do not count. Better to apply than to assume that you are not eligible. Also, you may be able to find free groceries or meals through churches or other community organizations (sometimes called "survival centers"). Consider shopping at discount grocery chains and bakery "thrift" shops.

What if you have no car or can't drive?

If you are on MassHealth, you may be eligible for transportation to medical appointments when you have no other alternatives. Monthly bus passes are offered at reduced rates to the disabled. If you cannot ride the regular bus, you may be eligible for van service.

If you live in Hampden or Hampshire counties, contact the Alliance for Injured Workers at 413-731-0760 to request a free copy of the *Injured Workers Survival Guide*, a directory of community resources in the area.

BUY IT FOR LESS!

Cosmetology schools often offer a wide range of low-cost services. If you are willing to let students practice cutting your hair, a haircut and blow dry could cost as little as $4 or $5.

A massage may seem like a luxury that you cannot afford. Try a massage therapy school.

Discount theater chains sell tickets for less. (You may have to wait a little longer for your favorite movie to get there, and the theater may lack stadium seating.)

You can find some decent clothes at Goodwill, the Salvation Army, consignment shops and survival centers.

Tag sales are an excellent place to find clothes and household items.

The local library can save you a tremendous amount of money. You can borrow movies and books. If the film or book you want is not at your local library, you can make a request for an inter-library loan. The movie will be shipped for pick up at your local library. If you cannot afford a computer, most libraries offer access to computers. You can sign up for free Internet service through Yahoo or Hotmail and access your email at the library.

CHAPTER 25

EMOTIONAL SURVIVAL

Try to get connected with a group of people that can support you and have gone through the same stuff.

It is not unusual for people with chronic medical problems to develop chronic emotional problems as well. Their lives often spiral downward. They have financial problems, so they start to worry. They become isolated. They may not be getting support from family and friends. Depression and anxiety are often the result.

How can you stop feeling so isolated?

Connect with other injured workers. Find other people who are in similar circumstances. Knowing that you are not alone will make a difference. If there is no support group for injured workers in your area, consider starting one. A local library or hospital may provide meeting space. You also may be able to meet people with disabilities through support groups at hospitals, advocacy organizations, and online disability networks.

How should you choose a therapist?

If you decide to see a professional therapist, ask questions during the first few sessions. Ask the therapist directly what he or she thinks of people who are not working. (You will be surprised by what people say in response to this question.) Search for someone who has experience treating patients with chronic medical conditions. Ask about confidentiality. Sometimes, therapy notes are passed on to insurers or are submitted as evidence for SSDI. Some therapists keep detailed notes; others keep very brief notes to preserve confidentiality. Request copies of your records. You will find out what the therapist thinks of you and whether or not there have been misunderstandings. A therapist's remarks may be so off base and damaging to your disability claim that you may need to find another one. (For example, you may discover that the therapist thinks you are a malingerer.)

Where can you turn when you are suicidal or desperate?

Most communities have a **crisis hotline.** The number is usually listed in the front of the phone book. Another option is going into a **psychiatric hospital.** We realize that you will probably consider this only as a last resort. Advocates for people labeled with mental illness have raised concerns about the treatment of patients in these institutions. The staff may not be knowledgeable or understanding about your medical condition. Once you are inside, you cannot simply walk out, even if you are considered a voluntary patient. Still, if you are suicidal or extremely depressed, or so angry that you are thinking of hurting someone, this may be the right choice for you.

There are alternatives to hospitals. These programs were developed partly because they are less expensive than inpatient hospitalization. They allow people to get intensive help without actually being confined to a hospital. **Partial hospitalization programs** are day programs that are usually connected to hospital psychiatric wards. You may attend for a few hours a day, for three or four days a week. The programs usually last several weeks. These programs are voluntary. You can stop going if you choose.

They may include group therapy sessions and educational presentations about a variety of topics, such as how to deal with stress. You usually need a referral from a psychiatrist or therapist to be admitted. Sitting for hours may be difficult, so discuss your limitations with the staff. These programs usually do not include one-on-one counseling. For financial reasons, they tend to rely on group therapy. As patients are leaving and entering the program at different intervals, you may not be with the same group each session. Some people are uncomfortable with the group model, while others find it helpful.

Respite centers are another alternative to hospitalization. You stay in a respite center 24 hours a day for several days. The environment is less restrictive than a hospital. Your stay in a respite center is voluntary, but while you are there, you will probably be expected to stay in the center 24 hours a day, or leave for short periods on passes. These centers typically have staff available to talk to you. A respite center is meant to provide a break from problems that are overwhelming you. **The staff at a respite center or partial hospitalization program can force you to go**

to a psychiatric ward if they believe that you are incapable of controlling suicidal impulses.

Can you find new goals and values?

Realizing that you will always have pain or limitations, and that you will never return to your career, can be devastating. As dark as this period of your life may be, please be aware that many disabled people eventually find ways to live a meaningful life. Although we feel a loss of identity initially, we realize that our self-worth exists apart from our jobs. We may even gain positive insight, valuing families and friends more than we did previously. You can find ways other than full-time work to contribute to society. Perhaps you are taking care of your family or helping other injured workers. Recognize and give yourself credit for your achievements. Surviving under extremely difficult circumstances is a far greater achievement than any professional accomplishment.

Perhaps you can channel some of the anger you feel about the system into changing it. Find out about changes in laws that are needed to help injured workers. Contact your state representative and senator and tell them what is wrong with the system. If they do not hear from us, they will not know that there is a problem. You may lift your own spirits by helping others. Network with disability rights groups.

I'm so scared of losing the support I do have. I spend a lot of time worrying about that.

----◆----

Figure out your mental health. A friend kept bugging me to get on anti-depressants. If I hadn't, I think I might have done something tragic. Depression is part of losing your livelihood, so don't be afraid to deal with that. I made a list of things I wanted to do, but never had time. Find an interest or a hobby, something you can get some enjoyment from. There's so much time when you're alone and really in pain. Find your own spiritual connection. For some people it's religion, yoga, or meditation. Some touchstone that keeps you balanced because it's really easy to stay in the dark place. Find a group of people in the same straits.

----◆----

I think it was with their help and support [friends and family] that made the difference. I had to do it, and I'm serious, through laughter. And I went and got help. I would suggest anyone else going through this go to counseling. My mental diagnosis is clinical depression, and in fact I still go see [my therapist] sometimes. I can vent things to her that I can't vent to my family because I don't want to burden them with it. Sometimes, I just want someone else that I can tell. And I'm on antidepressants. If I wasn't depressed, there would be something wrong with me. I'm sitting in a wheelchair. I can't do things. I can't breathe without oxygen. You would be surprised at the people who would put their hands out if you ask. I believe in karma, and there's a reason for everything. It just is, I can't figure out what this one was.

----◆----

Try to get support from family and friends, but you will be lucky if they understand what you're going through. Look for support from others who have been through a similar situation. Find someone, whether it's a counselor, or a church member, or even a friend who can sit and listen. You need some place to vent. It helped to know I wasn't by myself. Other people had gone through similar situations.

CHAPTER 26

UNIONS AND WORKERS COMP

People have this irrational sense of loyalty to their employer. To them, you're just a statistic. You're not a person to them. They don't see you as an individual. You are a number to fill a place, a body to fit the quota.

Union contracts can provide injured workers with benefits and protections that the law does not provide. Unions can also improve workplace safety by creating a health and safety committee. (The union may choose to create two committees, one focusing on prevention and the other on helping injured workers) If you belong to a union, contact your union or Western MassCOSH (or Mass-COSH) for ideas on how to make a committee work.

Tasks of a workers comp committee may include the following:

- Informing members of their rights.
- Filing grievances when an employee is harassed for filing a claim.
- Reviewing claims to identify hazards in the workplace.
- Locating sympathetic doctors who can identify and treat job-related injuries and illnesses.

- Assisting members in filing claims.
- Identifying reliable lawyers experienced in workers comp.
- Keeping in touch with and supporting injured members.
- Providing referrals for financial counseling.
- Providing testimony at legislative hearings.

What issues related to workers comp can a union negotiate?

The law says specifically that a union can negotiate the following:

- Benefits supplemental to sections 35, 34A, 35 and 36.
- An alternative dispute system, such as arbitration or mediation.
- The use of a limited list of providers for medical treatment.
- The use of a limited list of impartial physicians.
- The creation of light duty, modified job or return-to-work program.
- The adoption of 24-hour health care coverage plan.
- The establishment of safety committees and safety procedures.
- The establishment of vocational rehabilitation programs.

Arbitration

If the union and employer agree to arbitration, they must notify the DIA five days before the conference, and use a form called, "Agreement to Refer a Case to Arbitration." Both sides must agree that the arbitrator's award will address all issues under the workers comp law. The award is final and binding. Your union should insist that the employer or its insurer pay for the arbitrator. The union should also insist that the employer or its insurer pay the fees and expenses for the lawyer representing the injured worker, if the injured worker wins the arbitration.

Review Committee for Workers Comp Claims

The law allows for union and management to set up a claim review committee. This could reduce arbitration costs and lawyer's fees. Both sides would have to agree under what conditions (if any) a claim would go to arbitration. These committees are not always successful. If the union and employer have a history of resolving grievances fairly through joint boards, then it could work. If the history has been difficult and confrontational, then it could be a bad idea. If the committee cannot resolve the claim, it will just delay the claim. **A WORD OF CAUTION:** There is disagreement about whether unions should negotiate on alternative dispute resolution. Unions must be careful not to harm the rights and benefits of injured workers.

Suggested Contract Clauses to Protect Injured Union Members

Provide coverage for injuries not covered by workers comp:

"The company agrees to reimburse employees for all lost pay for occupational injuries and illnesses which cause less than five days of disability."

"The company agrees to reimburse employees for all lost pay for occupational injuries and illnesses to cover the first five days of disability when the disability is 20 days or less."

Cover time lost to see doctors and attend DIA proceedings:

"Any employee, who during working hours must see a doctor for treatment for an occupational injury or illness, or is a witness at a DIA conference or hearing, shall be paid for all time lost at his or her hourly rate."

Ensure continued medical and life insurance benefits

"Any employee who suffers an occupational injury or illness shall be considered an employee for the duration of disability, and the company will continue all insurance benefits during such period."

Provide continued seniority:

"An employee who suffers an occupational injury or illness shall continue to accrue seniority during the period of disability, and such time shall be considered worked for purpose of pension and vacation benefits."

Ensure an adequate income:

"The company agrees to pay employees receiving workers compensation a supplemental amount which, when added to weekly compensation, will equal the employee's net pay for the last full week worked before the disability commenced."

Notification of injuries:

"Promptly after the occurrence of any injury to an employee, the company shall furnish to the union a copy of the record of the initial visits to the company dispensary or to the doctor provided by the company and shall give the union one copy of each *First Report of Injury* form filed with the DIA."

Ensure continued employment:

"An employee who recovers from an occupational injury or illness shall be returned to his or her regular job."

Guarantee employment for partially disabled workers:

"Any employee unable to perform his or her regular work because of an occupational injury or illness shall be assigned a job the employee is able to perform if such work is available or held by another employee with less seniority."

Prevent discrimination:

"The company agrees not to discriminate in hiring or other conditions of employment against the handicapped or previously injured workers because of prior compensation claims."

Provide Sickness & Accident coverage in contested cases:

"In case of a disputed workers compensation claim, Sickness & Accident payment will be made during the interim period providing the employee signs an agreement to repay the Sickness & Accident insurer if he or she receives workers compensation for said period."

Penalize employer negligence:

"In any case in which an employee suffers an occupational injury or illness as a result of the company's violation of a recognized safety and/or health standard, rule or law, the company will provide a supplement to workers compensation in the amount of 25 percent of all weekly compensation payments."

CHAPTER 27

CHANGING THE WORKERS COMP LAW

How evil the system is as it's set up now.

The system is governed by the 1991 "reform" legislation. Changing it means changing the law. This could mean a major overhaul of the system, or changing pieces of it at a time. Either way, we face an uphill battle. Prejudice against injured workers and perceptions of widespread fraud have taken hold in the public imagination. Thousands of bills are introduced in the Legislature each term, but only a handful become law. Legislators are bombarded with requests for support for various causes. It takes many loud voices to rise above the "din." They will only hear our concerns if large numbers of us speak out.

What can you do to help?

The current system was not created by accident. It was put in place by legislators who voted to approve it. The people of Massachusetts voted to put those legislators in office. Here is what you can do to help:

- Call your legislator or visit during office hours. Your legislator needs to hear from you, even if nothing can be done immediately to resolve your problems. If additional constituents complain, eventually the message will be heard. If you do not know who represents you, check our website (www.afiw.org).

- Write a personal letter or email detailing your own experiences. (This is more effective than a form letter or mass email distributed to many people.)

- Find out where candidates stand on issues that are important to injured workers. For example, every two years, there is an election for the Governor's Council, the body that approves or rejects the governor's nominees for judges, including DIA judges. Not enough citizens pay attention to this election.

- Vote. Legislators may check to find out if you are a registered voter and whether or not you voted in the last election. They may not care about what you have to say if you do not vote.

General Reforms

I think I would change the whole system.

Here are some general reforms that have been supported by the Alliance for Injured Workers and our allies. Contact us to find out about pending legislation.

- Change scarring benefits so they are not limited to scars on the face, hands and neck.

- Index the maximum benefit for scarring to the state's annual average wage. The maximum benefit is now $15,000.

- Raise the benefit for funeral expenses from $4,000 to at least $7,000.

- Increase medical rates. (One proposal is to set them at 80 percent of the usual and customary charges for medical procedures.)

- Limit utilization review to the most frequent types of care given to injured workers. Current law allows for utilization review of every procedure, regardless of how trivial.

- Encourage insurers to follow utilization review time guidelines by automatically approving treatment when they fail to meet them. Current law requires a timely decision, but does not include any penalty.

- Require the general health insurer of the injured worker to cover medical expenses until the workers comp insurer is ordered to pay.

- Allow for an emergency conference before a judge to determine if an injured worker is entitled to medical treatment.

- Take away the prima facie status of the impartial physician report.

- Allow the administrative judge to appoint an impartial physician if he or she feels it is necessary, but do not require it.

- Make the impartial physician's opinion not binding on the judge and eliminate barriers to introducing treating physician reports.

- Restore maximum benefits to 66 2/3 of the pre-injury wage (up to the average weekly wage).

- Increase to ten the number of years that injured workers can collect for partial disability. The limit is now five years.

- Increase amounts for loss of function benefits.

CHAPTER 28

OTHER CHANGES THAT ARE NEEDED

I was really angry that I couldn't get food stamps. I couldn't get assistance. A lot of anger reared its ugly head. Here I am a contributor to society. I supported myself through school. I worked very hard to have a house and pay taxes, and the government and the state said, "We can't help you."

We have described some of the changes that we would like to see in workers comp law. Other changes, not specific to workers comp, would also benefit injured workers. You may now need help from programs that you once thought were only for "poor people." When these programs are cut, and the recipients dismissed as "freeloaders," injured workers are hurt, also. Many working people are only one major illness or injury away from financial disaster. These programs exist to help everyone.

How can we fix our health care system?

Much is wrong with our health care system. Many people are uninsured. Injured workers may lose their private health insurance once they stop working. Some injured workers do not qualify for Medicaid because their compensation income puts them just above the eligibility requirements. As a society, we need to provide every citizen with access to health care, regardless of the cause of the injury.

Under the current system, people who are injured are sometimes caught between insurers who are arguing over liability. Instead of just trying to get better, a sick person is expected to "prove" the cause of their condition. People who are hurt at work may have been injured before, and they may suffer from additional injuries or illnesses later in their lives. Insurers jump on these previous or subsequent injuries as if they have discovered a shameful secret. Having a complex medical history is part of being human.

One solution was mentioned in the last chapter: force the personal health insurer to cover treatment until a dispute over causation is resolved. Another possible solution is a single-payer health care system that would remove the question of liability.

> *Years after settling my workers comp case, I was in a car accident. When I went to see my doctor, the office manager yelled at me and said that I could not discuss the accident. I made some phone calls and got the necessary referral from the auto insurance. Then, she said I could discuss only the car accident and not my previous condition. "What if the car accident made my previous condition worse?" I asked. She had no answer. Another doctor told me that I would have to make separate appointments, on different days, to discuss the conditions covered by different insurances.*

How can doctors help?

We need to change the way doctors treat patients. Many injured workers have had good experiences, but others report encounters with arrogant and insensitive doctors. These negative experiences seem to happen more often when the patient is suffering from an occupational illness, such as multiple chemical sensitivity or repetitive strain injury.

Some doctors do not believe that these conditions are "real." They are skeptical of conditions that cannot be easily diagnosed, or are not old, well-established syndromes. They do not want to learn about, accept, or treat more complex conditions. Patients suffer greatly as a result of these attitudes. It is frightening to go to a doctor for help and to be met with hostility and suspicion, or to be told it is psychological.

Consider how different this experience is from that of someone who is treated for heart disease, diabetes or multiple sclerosis. Medical skepticism can make it difficult for injured workers to win their cases. Some impartial physicians have destroyed cases by doubting the existence of particular syndromes.

The law puts the burden on injured workers to "prove" the medical facts, but people with complex medical conditions are overwhelmed by dealing with debilitating health effects and financial difficulties. They do not have the expertise or the resources to "prove" that their condition is real. The medical profession and the courts must take the responsibility for researching and legitimizing these conditions.

> *I think I would change the way they are so biased toward certain illnesses. If they don't know what it is, they don't care, so they don't even want to learn about it.*

How can we provide a safety net for people who are disabled?

Just as there should be treatment available regardless of the cause of a medical condition, so should there be wage replacement. What happens to individuals who are injured at work but are not successful in proving it, or who have a medical condition unrelated to work? They fall through a gap in our state's safety net. Some can use sick time, but it will eventually run out. Others have no sick time or long-term disability. Unemployment benefits are designed for individuals who are able to work. Applicants for Social Security disability face a long, hard battle that could take years.

Some states have temporary disability programs. If we had that in Massachusetts, the psychological pressure on people going through the workers comp system would be less severe. Even if they did not succeed in "proving" their case, they would have some income.

Welfare benefits have been cut substantially. Some type of last resort financial assistance has to be available. Many injured workers do not qualify for welfare because they have too many assets (as would be expected after working for years). We should reconsider asset tests not just for welfare, but for other programs such as food stamps. The goal should be to help people maintain a certain standard of living, rather than force them to become destitute before we help them.

Final Thoughts

No one should have to experience the injustice, poverty, and emotional trauma that the injured workers quoted in this book have described. Many injured workers have been robbed not only of their physical health, but of their emotional well-being, also. The workers comp system causes as much pain as the injuries. Members of the Alliance for Injured Workers have been listening to, advising and comforting each other for more than a decade. The alliance is a collective triumph born out of personal tragedies.

A small group of thoughtful people could change the world. Indeed, it's the only thing that ever has.

Margaret Mead

SECTION II

FEDERAL WORKERS COMPENSATION

Contributed By Katherine Smith, Esq.

Based on
"Smith's Basic Survival Guide To Federal Workers Compensation"

INTRODUCTION

This section is taken from a short handbook entitled *Smith's Survival Guide to Federal Workers Compensation*. While that guide was meant to apply to workers all over the country, this section has been modified to cover only the basics and to apply especially to Massachusetts federal workers.

Do **not** rely on employers to give you a correct and complete answer to any question. They may not really know the answer, and there are probably no consequences to them if they give you wrong or incomplete information. If you don't find an answer that may apply to a specific question in this section, that does not mean there is no answer. You may need to contact a knowledgeable Union representative, a **federal** workers compensation attorney, or your Office of Workers' Compensation Programs (OWCP) Claims Examiner in Boston directly. The current contact numbers are included in this section.

It is important to state, at the very beginning of this section, that this is an extremely complicated area of law. Application of the statute is inconsistent and unpredictable. In some ways it is similar to the state's workers compensation system. However, some of the concepts are very different. One of the biggest differences is that there is no court review of the decisions. This is because the process is supposed to be non-adversarial. Another major difference is that **there are no additional punitive damages for negligence even if the federal employer intentionally ignored the risk and the resulting injury was foreseeable.** The Federal Employees Compensation Act (FECA) also makes it illegal for an attorney to take a case on a "contingency," or percentage, basis. Claimants always have to pay their own attorney's fees whether they win or lose. Employers and the OWCP never have to pay attorney's fees even if it is their fault that the claimant had to get an attorney. The thinking is that a lawyer should not be necessary because, again, it is supposed to be a non-adversarial process. The main reason for these differences is because there is no insurance company involved. Since there is no court review, there is no motivation to "settle." In fact, there is no mechanism to settle even if the Department of Labor or the employer wanted to do so. The Federal Government takes the role of employer, insurance company, and Appellant Judge. Make no mistake about it, the federal government guards its money just as strenuously as any insurance company. Since the Department of Labor's Employees' Compensation Appeals Board (ECAB) also has the absolute last say on whether you qualify for benefits for injury due to your federal employment, and there is no possibility of taking the ECAB to court, the system is slanted against you from the beginning.

Since there is no court review, decisions are often inconsistent. What works for one person today may not work for another person tomorrow. The application of many of the rules, policies, and procedures simply makes very little logical sense. This is a very basic summary of how it usually works. There is no way to cover every question and situation regarding federal workers compensation in an entire book much less a section of a book. However, this section is meant to give you a very basic idea of how it should work.

OVERVIEW

The Federal Employees' Compensation Act (FECA) can be found in the United States Code at 5 U.S.C. 8101. The regulations that apply to the administration of the act can be found in the Code of Federal Regulations (CFR) Title 20 Chapter 1 in Part 10. In Massachusetts, the FECA is administered by the Department of Labor through the Office of Workers' Compensation Programs (OWCP), Boston District Office. Appeals are made to the Branch of Hearings and Review in Washington, DC. Final appeals are made to the Employees' Compensation Appeals Board (ECAB). Addresses can be found on page 170.

The phone number for the Boston District Office is currently 617-624-6600. Unless you are just asking a general question regarding whether something is in the file or the status of your claim, you will probably just want to dial #9 and leave a voicemail message for your Claims Examiner to call you back rather than waiting to leave a message with the person answering the phone. That person will only be able to answer simple questions regarding what is currently in your file and will not have the power to make any decisions in your case. Although calls are supposed to be returned within three days, you may need to be persistent if you want to speak directly to your Claims Examiner. You may need to call once or twice a week until the call is returned.

Written correspondence for all the District Offices is routed through an imaging house in London, KY[1], where it is put into digital form and transmitted to the District Offices. As you can probably guess, this creates a predictable bottleneck. Digital files seem like a good idea in theory; in practice, it turns out that it is very difficult to accurately maintain and work from a digital file. A number of Claims Examiners and Hearing Representatives have admitted to me that digital files are extremely difficult to work with and the new decision making hierarchy makes it very difficult to make decisions in a timely fashion. While the new system may help eliminate fraud on the part of the Claims Examiners, and may make accountability more possible, it slows down the process and makes it even more difficult for them to do their job.

Claims Examiners and Hearing Representatives have also complained that the software (iFECS) that is used to access the files has been full of bugs (reported to be over 4,300 as of 1/1/06). Claims Examiners have also complained that rather than fix the bugs, they have been forced to figure out a way to work around them. It can take weeks for a document to make it into the imaged file. If it is not properly tagged, the Claims Examiner or Hearing Representative may not even be aware that there is new documentation in the file, or that an appeal or request for reconsideration has been filed, until the injured worker calls to request the status of the claim. Hearing Representatives are sometimes forced to

---

1   It is interesting to note that the Elaine Chao, the Secretary of the Department of Labor, is married to Mitch McConnell who was a Republican Senator from Kentucky serving as a senior member of the Appropriations Committee and Senate majority whip when the contract was awarded.

print out the entire file so that the claim can be worked on more easily. It is a good idea to call after a week or so and verify that any documentation that you send has been scanned into the file and reviewed by the Claims Examiner or hearing representative.

Authorization for treatment and payment of medical bills for all of the injured workers in the country through all of the District Offices is done by a private contractor called ACS which is currently located in Florida.[2] Their website is: http://owcp.dol.acs-inc.com/portal/main.do. They are located at:

ACS EDI Gateway, Inc.
2324 Killearn Center Blvd.
Tallahassee, FL 32309
1-800-987-6717

To speak with a Customer Service Representative regarding an authorization, you have to call 850-558-1818 which will be a toll call from Massachusetts. Since most authorizations have to be done by, and through, your doctor, there is usually no point in calling ACS. If you have problems with Prescription Benefits and Processing questions, you have to call ACS at 866-664-5581. Again, the doctor or pharmacist will probably have to call. If you do end up paying for something that is later approved out of your own pocket, you may request reimbursement on a medical

---

2   Is the connection between this very large contract with the federal agency and the state of Florida a coincidence?

reimbursement form provided by your Claims Examiner upon your request.

Each employer is supposed to have at least one "Point Person." The Postal Service calls them "Injury Compensation Specialists." Other agencies such as the Veterans Administration (VA) and the Transportation Safety Agency (TSA) usually designate someone in Human Relations (HR) to function as an OWCP point person. They work for the employer, and **they do not have the power to make any decisions regarding your claim**. Although most of the paperwork has to be submitted through them, they are only there to answer questions, facilitate limited duty accommodations, and to pass along the paperwork. They are supposed to be there to help you. Although some of these people are conscientious and helpful, most of them have no motivation to give you complete and accurate information. Take what they say with a grain of salt. **If you need a definite answer to your question, call your Claims Examiner in Boston. Claims examiners are the only ones who have power to make a decision regarding your claim.**

The FECA is a complicated statute that is extremely difficult for even a reasonably intelligent and educated person to navigate successfully. Proceedings under the Act are not supposed to be adversarial. You are not supposed to need a lawyer in order to get your benefits. Although you have the burden of proving that you are entitled to compensation, OWCP is supposed to share in the responsibility to develop the evidence. They are not supposed to simply deny a claim because you did not know how to present it properly. OWCP is supposed to meet its obligation to see that justice is done. <u>Buck Jordan</u>, 94-1662 (4/3/96); <u>William J. Cantrell</u>,

34 ECAB 1233 (1983); <u>Gertrude E. Evans</u>, 26 ECAB 195 (1974); FECA Procedure Manual Chapter 2-810 (8). However, we all know that things do not always work the way they are supposed to work.

Who Is Covered?

The FECA statute covers civilian federal employees (with the exception of non-appropriated fund employees). This includes employees of the Postal Service, IRS, Social Security Administration, Veterans Administration, Fish and Game, and many others. Probationary, temporary, part-time, seasonal, intermittent, and term employees are all covered from the first day of work. Special Legislation has also provided coverage for Peace Corps and Vista Volunteers as well as Job Corps, Neighborhood Youth Corps, Youth Conservation Corps, enrollees, Federal Grand and Pettit Jurors, volunteer members of the Civil Air Patrol, and Reserve Officer Training Corps Cadets. Non federal law enforcement officers are sometimes covered in situations involving crimes against the United States. You are covered from the first day you start work.

Can I Sue My Employer For Negligence?

The short answer is No! FECA is a "no fault" statute which means that, generally, it makes no difference whether your injury is your fault or the employer's as long as you didn't purposely hurt yourself. It also means that you cannot sue your employer for pain and suffering due to an injury caused by negligence or emotional distress caused by their mistakes. Under very limited circumstances, you may be compensated for lost time due to an emotional injury diagnosed by a psychiatrist. "Stress" claims are extremely difficult and will be discussed later in greater detail. There is no increase in benefits even if the employer's intentional negligence caused the injury. Injured workers cannot sue their supervisors individually as long as their actions arc **arguably** part of their job! So again, the answer is no. You cannot sue your employer or, in most cases, a coworker, for negligence, even if you can prove that it is intentional, and caused your injury. However, if the injury was caused by a subcontractor, a work-related motor vehicle accident, a dog bite, or a slip and fall due to a negligent postal customer or any other third party (not your employer or coworker), you may be able to sue the third party for personal injury.

How Do I File A Claim?

Is there a time limit when filing a claim?

Yes. You must file a claim within three years of the day that you are aware, or reasonably **should** have been aware, that your condition was work related. In the case of a CA-1 (traumatic injury) this means that you must file the claim within three years of the incident that caused the injury. However, you should note that the time starts to run as of the time that you become **aware** that your injury is related to your job.

For example: A federal employee is severely traumatized when he sees a coworker crushed by a forklift. He had been sober for ten years but as a result of the trauma, he starts drinking again. His job performance suffers. He loses his job and his house. It never occurs to him, or anyone else, that his worsening depression and anxiety is related to what he had witnessed at work. It is five years later when his psychiatrist finally attributes his PTSD to seeing his coworker injured.

After a five-year downward spiral he finally starts to get treatment. He files a claim for a traumatic emotional injury caused by witnessing the accident at work. His doctors support him. They report that he could no longer work for the federal agency in any capacity because he could not even enter the building without aggravating his PTSD. His claim is accepted as work-related PTSD even though the actual event happened more than five years before. He finally receives the help he needed and is on the way to recovery.

What Compensation Can I Get?

If the claim is accepted and you are totally disabled, you will receive **66.6%** of your pay if you have no dependents and **75%** if you are married or have dependents. Shift differential and holidays are included as part of your pay. **Overtime is not included.** If you were working full time at the date of injury and you are only able to work part-time because of your work-related injury, OWCP will pay 75% or 66.6% of the difference between your pre-injury wage and your part-time wage.

If you were a volunteer (e.g., Peace Corps, Corp and Vista Volunteers as well as Job Corps, Neighborhood Youth Corps, Youth Conservation Corps, enrollees, Federal Grand and Pettit Jurors, volunteer members of the Civil Air Patrol Job Corps) when you were injured, your compensation will be based on the minimum, which is the current basic monthly salary for a GS-2. If you were a temporary, part-time, seasonal, intermittent, or term employee when you got injured, your benefits will be based on your actual salary or the salary of a GS-2, whichever is greater.

Your compensation is based on the number of hours in your regular job description. If you do not have regular hours, (e.g., a part-time flexible postal employee), your compensable hours will probably be figured as the average weekly hours that you worked the year previous to your date of injury. It is not subject to income tax.

There is no possibility for a settlement. You get compensated only for lost time and possibly a set amount according to your percentage of permanent impairment to certain parts of the body (Schedule Award).

What is Continuation Of Pay (COP)?

If you have an accepted claim for traumatic injury you should receive Continuation Of Pay (COP) from your employer for the first 45 days that you miss work.[3] COP is 100% of your pay and is subject to the regular deductions and taxes. It is simply, as the name suggests, a continuation of your pay. The 45 days do not have to be consecutive, but they do have to fall within the first 90 days after the injury.

---

3   Congress is currently considering an amendment to the statute that would allow the Postal Service to require a three day waiting period before starting to pay COP unless disability exceeds 15 days.

If you file a CA-1 for a traumatic injury more than 30 days after the incident that caused the injury, the Employer may refuse to give you COP until after the claim is accepted. If you are receiving COP, and your claim is denied, the employer may demand that you change your COP to sick or annual leave. If you don't have any sick or annual leave left, the employer may ask you to pay the money back out of future wages or Disability Retirement benefits. This can happen even if you appeal the denial. If you win the appeal, you may get that compensation back.

Third Party Claims

If your injury was caused by a third party, not an employee of your federal employer, you actually may be required to either sue that person yourself or sign the right to sue over to OWCP or your employer. The most common examples of this are dog bites (postal workers), motor vehicle accidents while on duty, and slips and falls while on duty but walking off of federal property (e.g., letter carriers on their route).

It is usually better to look for a personal injury attorney that will take the case on contingency and sue yourself. **However, most personal injury lawyers do not know that a good part of any settlement will go to paying back the federal government.**

You should try to find an attorney who has some experience with settlements involving third party claims in federal workers compensation cases. The Attorney must fill out the following statement and submit it with a reimbursement check.

STATEMENT OF RECOVERY

(1) Amount of Gross Recovery ....$ _____

(2) Amount for Property Damage, if any.........................$ _____

(3) Balance (Line 1 minus (-) Line 2)................................$ _____

(4) Amount Allocated for Loss of Consortium...................$ _____
     (___% of Line 3)

(5) Balance (Line 3 minus Line 4) ....$ _____

(6) Amount for Wrongful Death or Survival ....$ _____
     (circle one). Line 6 is _____ % of Line 5.

(7) Balance (Line 5 minus Line 6) ....$ _____

(8) Less Attorney's Fee (Fee is _____% of line 7).......$ _____

(9) Balance ....$ _____

(10) Less Court Costs ....$ _____

(11) Balance (adjusted gross recovery) ....$ _____

(12) Enter 20% of amount on Line 11 ....$ _____

(13) to Balance (Line 11 minus Line 12) ....$ _____

(14) Enter OWCP Disbursements of....................................$ _____
     or amount on Line 13 above, whichever is less

(15) Government Allowance for Attorney's Fee ....$ _____
     to pursue OWCP claim (retained by claimant)

(16) Balance (Line 14 - Line 15) Refund To Owcp.............$ _____

(17) Surplus (line 13 - line 14) Credit Against Future Benefit).........$ _____

As the form suggests, if you have a surplus, OWCP will not pay any bills until the amount of the bills or lost time exceeds the amount of the surplus. If you end up with a surplus, you should keep track of the bills so you will know when you should start receiving compensation again.

WHAT FORM SHOULD I USE?

The type of claim that you file depends on the **cause** of your current **disability**, not necessarily the cause of the original injury. Keep in mind that a temporary or permanent **aggravation** of a prior condition, whether the prior condition is work related or not, may be compensable under the Federal Employees' Compensation Act (FECA). There are three forms on which a claim may be filed:

1.) CA1 – Traumatic Injury

If the injury was caused or aggravated by a specific *incident* on a single shift, you should file a CA1. The medical evidence must focus on a single incident that caused or aggravated your condition causing the current disability. One advantage to defining a claim as a traumatic injury is that you are entitled to Continuation of Pay (COP) for 45 days after the first day of disability. COP is paid at 100% (taxed) rather than the 66.6% or 75% (untaxed) rate that applies to regular continuing compensation benefits. A disadvantage to defining disability as caused by a specific incident is that the disability from the specific incident may be found to be temporary.

If the underlying occupational injury remains unaccepted, OWCP may find that disability from the specific incident has ceased and terminate benefits even if disability from the underlying work-related condition still exists. You may claim **both** an aggravation from a single incident (CA1) **and** an underlying condition from job duties (CA2). However, if possible, it should not be done at the same time since having two open claims can be confusing to you as well as to the doctors and Claims Examiners.

2.) CA2- Occupational Injury

If the disability is from an injury that developed over time from *specific job duties*, over more than one shift, that caused or aggravated an injury you should file a CA2. *There is no COP for an occupational injury.*

You must provide an employee statement that says exactly what your specific job duties were when you were injured (e.g., extensive hand writing, computer work, data processing, filing, sorting mail, "sweeping" mail, lifting and positioning patients, repeated lifting, stooping or twisting, driving, walking a mail route and/or carrying a mail bag). Again, the injury must have happened over more than one shift. If the injury happened within one day, it would be filed on a CA1.

Your doctor must demonstrate knowledge of those same job duties, their duration, and their physical requirements. Then the doctor must explain exactly how each job duty caused or aggravated your condition. Keep in mind that if any part of the doctor's opinion turns out to be based on inaccurate information, the entire opinion may be found invalid and the claim may be denied.

Sometimes the initial injury does not become obvious until the symptoms are so bad that they prevent you from working. A prior position may be the actual cause of an injury, the employer may accommodate the injured employee, and the condition may get worse anyway. The employer will try to argue that the condition is not work related because the limited/light duty job could not have caused or aggravated the injury. If this happens, the doctor must relate the current disability to the prior job.

For example: An employee does data entry for eight years and develops Carpal Tunnel Syndrome (CTS). The employer is made aware of her condition and a sympathetic supervisor has her answering the telephone and performing reception duties. She doesn't file a claim because she is able to work on the reception desk with no real problem.

However, six months later, she has a new supervisor who will not accommodate her and demands that she return to her old data entry job. She files a workers compensation claim. The claim is denied because OWCP says that she cannot prove that her receptionist duties caused or aggravated her CTS.

In this case the doctor was asked to write a letter clearly stating that the injury actually happened when the employee was performing the old data entry job and that she is still suffering from the condition. This would link the injury to the original data processing job which was the actual cause of the CTS rather than trying to argue that it was the receptionist duties that caused the injury.

Even when the claim was accepted, this employee would not receive any money unless she actually lost time from work **because** of physical restrictions from her accepted work-related injury. Since she initially did not lose any time for the first six months, she would not be compensated for that time period. However, she would be compensated for time that she lost because the employer couldn't, or wouldn't, offer her a position within her restrictions.

The doctor came through with a letter linking the employee's current condition with her past job duties and she was awarded benefits for the time that she lost because the new supervisor would not accommodate her restrictions due to her CTS which was found to be an accepted work-related injury.

1) CA2a- Recurrence of Disability

True recurrences of disability are relatively rare. **You can only file a claim of recurrence of disability due to a prior *accepted injury* with no aggravation from intervening factors** (including job duties). If you have disability due to an injury to the same part of the body, it will not necessarily qualify as a recurrence of disability unless it is caused by:

- a spontaneous material worsening of an *accepted* condition with no aggravation from any other incidents or activities in or out of work.

- the development of disability due to a new condition as a consequence of the *accepted* condition.

- authorized treatment or surgery due to the *accepted* condition.

- a material change in job duties that makes it impossible to do the job because of medical restriction due to the *accepted* condition.

- a withdrawal of a limited duty position because of restrictions from the *accepted* condition.

The most common examples of a recurrence of disability would be the following:

An employee with an accepted work-related injury is able to return to a limited duty position that is within the employee's restrictions. The employee is able to work in this position for some time. However, due to the natural progression of the accepted injury, the symptoms get worse and worse until the worker is unable to work at all. The injury would have gotten worse whether the employee was working or not. The job duties are not what actually made it worse (material worsening of accepted condition).

An injured employee with an accepted work-related **right** rotator cuff tear is forced to accept a limited duty position that requires performance of job duties with the **left** arm only. The injured worker develops CTS and tendonitis in the left arm and wrist as a result of overuse of the left arm (consequential injury).

After many years, an injured worker develops a severe work-related injury as the result of job duties. It is accepted as a work-related injury. Suddenly, the worker's career is cut short because of inability to do the job. Many injured workers need some kind of counseling, and they should not hesitate to get help dealing with the depression and anxiety that comes with a sudden, necessary, and substantial change in lifestyle. The injured worker becomes depressed and anxious as a result of the effects of the physical restrictions due to the injury. Major Depression and/or Anxiety due to physical restrictions imposed by an accepted work-related injury are extremely common. If it is diagnosed by a psychologist or psychiatrist, and results in an inability to continue working, an emotional condition may be considered a recurrence of disability (consequential injury).

An injured worker is able to work in a limited duty position within restrictions but becomes totally disabled while recovering from an authorized surgery or other medical treatment (total disability as a consequence of the injury).

An employer's change of policy and/or personnel results in a change in the employee's position. The employee is given duties that are outside of his or her medical restrictions and so is unable to work. This causes a recurrence of disability since the position is no longer within the injured worker's medical restrictions (material change in job).

An employer's change of policy and/or personnel results in the withdrawal of an injured worker's limited duty position which causes a recurrence of disability since the injured worker's position is no longer within specified medical restrictions (material change in job or withdrawal of limited duty job).

It is important to understand that a CA2a "recurrence" is **a recurrence of disability** *not* **a recurrence of the injury or an injury to**

the same part of the body. If the accepted injury is aggravated by your work, it is a new claim. If the injury was aggravated over more than one shift, the claim should be filed as a CA-2 (aggravation of prior condition by job duties). If there is another specific incident, such as lifting something or reaching, that aggravates your prior accepted injury, it is probably another CA-1 (aggravation of a prior condition by a specific incident).

Supervisors, and even point personnel, often make the mistake of advising employees to file a recurrence simply because they have injured the same part of the body that they had injured before. Since there are often intervening incidents or job duties, these claims are often denied without proper development even though the Claims Examiner is supposed to develop the claim according to the evidence and not according to the form it was filed on. However, it is easier for the Claims Examiner to simply deny the claim because the injured worker has not proven that there was an actual recurrence of disability as defined by FECA rather than properly develop the claim according to the evidence in the file. This is what usually happens if a claim is mistakenly filed as a recurrence rather than a new claim. It is sometimes easier to just file a new claim. However, if it is too late to do that because it has been more than three years since the aggravation, you may need to ask that the claim be "converted" to a CA-1 or a CA-2. If the Claims Examiner is not cooperative at this point, you probably need to find a federal workers compensation attorney.

3.) Expansions

When you receive an acceptance letter, it is extremely important to make sure that the injury that is accepted is the same as the injury that your doctor has currently diagnosed. **Your accepted injury is limited to what the acceptance letter says unless the claim is formally expanded.** OWCP often accepts an initial diagnoses that is less severe rather than the actual currently diagnosed injury as work related. The most common examples of this are the "lumbar strain" and "cervical strain" as opposed to herniated discs or a permanent aggravation of herniated discs. As a result of the incomplete initial acceptance of the work-related injury, future compensation for lost time and treatment may be denied since they are related to the more serious, but unaccepted, injury. It is important to understand that just because a doctor determines that the injury is actually more serious, OWCP does not automatically accept the final diagnosed injury as work-related.

For example, if an injury that was initially diagnosed, and accepted as a work-related lumbar strain turns out to be a herniated disc at L4-5, you must request that the claim be expanded to include the herniated disc before surgery or any other treatment for the herniated disc to be authorized.

Another example is a shoulder condition that is initially accepted as a "cervical strain" or "shoulder strain." An MRI shows that the injury is actually a torn rotator cuff. It may be necessary to request that the claim be expanded before surgery to include a torn rotator cuff. It will probably also be necessary to expand the claim before requesting a Schedule Award (permanent impairment award) since there is usually no permanent impairment from a strain.

To expand your claim, you must provide "bridging information" from your doctor. **Your doctor must provide an *unequivocal* opinion linking your *accepted* condition to your *current diagnosis*.** This kind of documentation is also necessary in a claim for a consequential injury.

4.) Consequential Injuries

The ECAB provided the best explanation of what it considers a "consequential injury" in their decision in the case of <u>Dennis J. Lasanen</u>, 41 ECAB 933 (1990). (See also <u>Margarette B. Rogler</u>, 43 ECAB 1034 (1992)). It says:

> When the primary injury is shown to have arisen out of and in the course of employment, every natural consequence that flows from the injury likewise arises out of the employment, unless it is the result of an independent intervening cause attributable to a claimant's own intentional conduct. The basic rule is that a subsequent injury, whether an aggravation of the original injury or a new and distinct injury, is compensable if it is the direct and natural result of a compensable primary injury.

It is a little more complicated than it sounds. The most common example of a consequential injury is "consequential depression." This injury is described above. In those cases, there must be medical documentation from a psychiatrist and/or a licensed Psychologist linking the emotional condition to the *pain and/or physical restrictions due to the accepted injury.* **It is very important to understand that emotional conditions**

caused by the way an injured employee is treated by the agency or OWCP will probably not be considered compensable. In order to support a claim for Consequential Depression, *the depression and/or anxiety must be linked to the pain and/or physical restrictions due to the accepted injury, and **not the behavior of anyone else.***

Another common consequential injury is due to overuse of another part of the body to compensate for the part that is injured. If you are forced to work with your left arm only because of an accepted injury to the right arm, you may develop an injury to the left arm as well. This could be characterized as either a consequential injury (CA-2) or as a new occupational injury (CA-2a). It is usually best to speak to the Claims Examiner to find out which one to file.

The same idea extends to all other consequential injuries. There *must* be strong, unequivocal, medical evidence linking the new condition to the accepted condition or any authorized treatment for that condition.

MEDICAL DOCUMENTATION

OWCP will probably not contact your doctor to get medical information! **It is *your* responsibility to provide the medical documentation to support your claim!** Medical documentation, from a medical doctor, not a chiropractor or a physicians assistant (PA), is *always necessary* for the claim to be accepted.

The best way to get good medical documentation is to take the following steps:

1.) Make a list of your job duties (at the time of injury) describing them in detail (CA2). You may even need to act out your job duties for your doctor so that the doctor understands the physical requirements of your job.

2.) Write a memo of all circumstances surrounding the incident that you believe caused current disability. (CA1)

3.) Be careful not to use language that is specific to your job without making sure that your doctor understands what you are saying.

4.) Take the list or memo to your doctor and ask for an opinion on whether the incident or job duties caused *or* aggravated your condition.

5.) If so, ask for a report that ties the specific job duties or incident (including the circumstances and date) to the diagnosed injury.

The OWCP requires specific information to approve a claim. At minimum, medical documentation must include the following:

1) A clear medical **diagnosis**.

2) A **history** of circumstances surrounding the injury, either from the patient or prior medical reports, (including the specific duties of the job that caused, or aggravated, the injury). **If the doctor does not demonstrate accurate and consistent knowledge of the history of the injury, OWCP may simply dismiss the doctor's opinion as not being based on accurate facts.**

3) **Treatment** history, including any symptoms, tests, and physical find-

ings and referral reports.

4) Acknowledgement of all **prior injuries** distinguishing any disability from those conditions from the disability due to the work-related injury.

5) **Prognosis** stating whether the disability is partial or total and whether it is temporary or permanent.

6) And, most importantly, **an opinion on causation**. It is important to relate the injury to a specific incident (CA-1), job duties (CA-2) or accepted injury (CA-2a). **OWCP will ignore opinions qualified with words such as "probably," "usually," "could have" or "may have" caused. Reports commencing with "It is my medical opinion that..." are given their full probative value.** The doctor also needs to provide a clearly stated medical rationale for an opinion that the injury was caused or aggravated by a specific incident (CA-1) or your specific job duties (CA-2) on that specific date.

DO NOT RELY ON YOUR DOCTORS TO PROVIDE THIS INFORMATION ON THEIR OWN! Most doctors will not provide this information unless you ask them to do so. It is very rare for doctors to get it right the first time. They need to understand how to frame their opinions, and it is often difficult to convince them that their opinions will be misused or ignored if they do not pay attention to the requirements of OWCP. The requirements of a request to expand a claim and for a claim for consequential injury are outlined above.

In the case of occupational injury claims, it is usually best to get the doctor's statement *first* and *then* fill out the CA2. That way you can be sure that your claim is consistent with the medical evidence. If you have already filled out the claim, make sure your doctor sees a copy so that his or her report can consistently support what you put on your claim form and in your employee statement. **Consistency is extremely important!** Your employee statement, claim form, and medical documentation must describe the same incident or cite the same job duties!

It is always best to get medical documentation of a traumatic injury (CA1) as soon as possible. The CA-1 should be filled out as soon as possible after the "incident" that caused, or aggravated, the injury. The claim must be filed within 30 days of the injury in order to get your continuation of pay by your employer for the first 45 days. A delay in seeking medical care could also result in a finding that there is insufficient evidence to show that the injury took place in the time, place and manner that you said it did.

Keep in mind that your employer will read the claim form (CA-1) or your employee statement (CA-2) and will object if they do not think it is accurate. If your employer can prove that your description of your job duties is not accurate, it will severely injure your credibility and the claim may be denied because the Claims Examiner may find that the injury did not occur "in the time, place, and manner alleged."

It is difficult to get witnesses to an incident to come forward if the employer says that the incident didn't happen the way you said it did (CA-1). It is also really difficult to prove that your job duties are actually not what is on your written job description as interpreted by your employer (CA-2). It is best to make sure that your description of an incident, or your employee statement regarding your job duties, cannot be challenged for accuracy because it will also undermine your medical evidence if your doctor demonstrates inaccurate knowledge of the circumstances surrounding an incident at work, or your actual job duties. Once you and your doctor lose credibility, it is very difficult to turn the claim around and get it approved.

HOW DO I RESPOND TO OWCP?

When you receive a letter from OWCP, it is extremely important to read it very carefully and respond appropriately if necessary. There are rules regarding how a claim is developed. The rules often give the claimant the chance to provide all the information necessary to get the claim approved. However, the claimant often doesn't know what the Claims Examiner is requesting. If OWCP needs more information, they may be required to further develop the evidence. Just read the letters very carefully and give them what they request. You may need to show the letter to your doctor. **Do not assume that the information is already in the record. READ THE LETTER CAREFULLY AND RESPOND IF NECESSARY!!** Follow these steps:

1.) You may receive a letter that says something like *"the evidence in the file is insufficient to determine if you have a medical condition related to your job duties. Please provide the following information within the next 30 days."* This is called a **development letter. It is extremely important to read and respond to these letters.**

2.) Check to see if the letter is addressed to you or someone else. OWCP often sends copies of letters sent to employers, doctors, or attorneys. If the letter is not addressed to you, it is probably not necessary to respond.

3.) If the letter is an **acceptance letter**, make sure the accepted injury is complete and accurate. **You will only be compensated for disability due to the *accepted* injury.** (E.g., if a claim is accepted for carpal tunnel syndrome in your right wrist, and you have permanent impairment and medical expenses for your right elbow, you will not be compensated for medical expenses or receive a schedule award for permanent impairment of the elbow even though the injury may have been caused by the same repetitive job duties and your doctor considers it the same injury, because the elbow injury is not part of the accepted claim.) Also follow the appropriate procedures in the section entitled "What To Do If Your Claim Is Accepted."

4.) If the claim is denied, follow the procedures in the Section "What To Do If Your Claim Is Denied."

WHAT DO I DO IF MY CLAIM IS DENIED?

1) *Note the **date** of the decision.* The clock on the appeal rights begins on that date.

2) Check the **number** of the claim to make sure it is correct.

3) Read the **appeal rights** on the last pages.

4) Read the **issues** that the decision is addressing.

5) **Highlight each conclusion** the Claims Examiner makes. (E.g., "the doctor's opinion was not probative because it was not rationalized" or "there was no medical evidence on the cause of the injury" or "the claimant failed to cite a compensable factor of employment" or "there is no evidence that the event actually took place in the time, place and manner alleged.")

6) **Highlight any factual errors.**

7) Request an Oral **Hearing** if it is the first denial. A hearing representative will consider new evidence.

8) **Address each conclusion** made against you with new evidence or explanation.

9) **Address each factual error** with objective evidence if possible.

10) Show the denial to your doctor and request a **medical report** that addresses all the highlighted issues.

11) Request **reconsideration** if you can get new medical evidence.

12) If you cannot get any new medical evidence and are not entitled to a hearing, file an ECAB appeal. **THIS IS USUALLY A LAST RESORT AND THE LAST STEP.** *The ECAB will not consider new evidence!*

•   **BEWARE! If you request reconsideration, but fail to submit *new and relevant* medical evidence or new legal arguments, your request for reconsideration may be denied. If the last merit review was more than a year ago, the ECAB may not review the merits of your claim!**

APPEAL RIGHTS

A denial will include the following appeal rights.

- **Oral Hearing Or A Review Of The Written Record**

  If this is the first denial, and it had been less than 30 days since the date of the decision, you may request an *oral hearing or a review of the written record by a Hearing Representative.* This option takes a long time. It currently takes 6-8 months to get a hearing date. However, it may be good to have the claim reviewed by a *Hearings Representative* out of Washington, DC, because they are usually more experienced and are outside of the District Office. You may present new evidence and/or argument at a hearing. It is an informal setting (usually a conference room). You have the opportunity to bring witnesses if you want to do so. Representatives from your employer may come and observe the hearing, but they may not participate. The hearing is recorded, so a recording technician is also present. You and the employer will receive a transcript of the hearing and will have an opportunity to respond in writing before a decision is made. Unless you request a different location, hearings requested by Massachusetts residents will generally be scheduled in Boston. However, for some Massachusetts residents, the federal building in Hartford, Connecticut, may be more convenient.

- **Reconsideration Request**

You can request **reconsideration** of your claim due to new medical evidence or legal argument within one year of the last decision on the merits of your claim. This is a good choice if you have new medical information and/or a new legal argument. It is best not to wait until the last moment in case the District Office refuses to conduct a merit review and you have to go to the ECAB. If it has been more than a year from the last decision on the merits, the ECAB cannot review the merits of the case. They will only determine if the District Office correctly refused to reconsider the claim. If the refusal is found to be justified, and it has been more than a year since the last merit review, you are done with that claim.

- **ECAB Appeal**

You have 90 days to file an **Appeal with the Employees' Compensation Appeals Board** (ECAB) (This can be extended to one year from the last merit decision for good cause. This includes a delay due to efforts to get new medical documentation for a reconsideration.) This option is a good choice only if there is no chance of getting any more medical evidence and you have no new legal arguments, or if there is a chance that the District Office will refuse to reconsider your claim on the merits, and you are close to the one year deadline for a review on the merits.

WHAT DO I DO IF MY CLAIM IS ACCEPTED?

Why Do I Have To Buy Back Sick And Annual Leave?

You don't. But you will not get it back unless you do. And you will not be paid for it again either. The FECA allows the individual Employing Federal Agency to determine its own policy regarding whether it will allow you to buy back any sick or annual leave that you used while your claim was being decided. (If you are entitled to COP, your leave should be converted automatically, and the leave buy back would not start until after the 45 days were used.) If your Agency allows "leave buy back," you will have to pay them the difference between what OWCP would pay you and the 100% of your wage that you got from the employer when you used the sick or annual leave. Here are two examples:

1.) Persons with no dependents will get 66.6 percent of their wages as OWCP benefits. They can convert the sick and/or annual that they used due to their accepted injury to OWCP benefits if they pay the employer the other 33.3%.

2.) An injured federal worker has a wife and children. The worker will receive 75% of his date of injury wage as OWCP benefits. When the claim is accepted, the worker can convert the sick and/or annual leave that was taken due to the accepted injury to OWCP benefits by paying the Agency back for the additional 25% received as sick and/or annual pay. **(It should be noted that leave is taxed whereas OWCP benefits are not.)**

You will need to file a CA-7b. **If you do not buy back your leave, you will not be compensated by OWCP for the sick and annual leave that you took because of your injury before the claim was accepted!** You cannot usually buy back leave taken after the claim has been accepted and you will not be compensated for it by OWCP either!

Continuation Of Pay (Cop)

If the claim is a traumatic injury (CA1), you should receive continuation of pay (COP) at 100% for the first **45 days** of disability. They can be intermittent, but any part of the day counts against the 45-day limit. *There is no COP for a CA-2 claim!*

CA-7 - Claim For Continuing Compensation

After your claim is accepted, you have to fill out a CA-7 in order to receive compensation for any time that you have missed. Ask your supervisor or OWCP point person for the CA-7. You fill out the first page, make yourself a copy, take the attached CA-20 to give to your doctor, and return the CA-7 to the employer. Make sure you make yourself a copy. The employer should fill out the other side of the form and send it on to OWCP within five days. Your doctor should fill out the attached CA-20. You can ask the doctor to give it back to you so you can submit it with the CA-7. Some doctors want to send it directly to OWCP. In either case, ask them to make you a copy.

A CA-7 may be filed any time after the claim has been accepted. **However, you will not be paid until you file a CA-7.** There is no hard, fast rule regarding what time frame you should use when you can file a claim for compensation on a CA-7. The first one usually covers any lost time between the date of injury (or when the COP ran out) and the date of acceptance. However, it is sometimes a good idea to separate the lost time into blocks according to whether you were totally out of work or were out intermittently or worked part-time onto separate CA-7s. **Do not overlap time periods when filling out CA-7s!** You can only claim a time period once. It is recommended that you file a CA-7 every two weeks or so after the first one until you go back to work or they put you on the Periodic Role. If disability is expected to last for a while, you may be put on the Periodic Role (PR). If you are put on the PR, you will be notified that you will not be required to file CA-7s and you should receive a check every 28 days or so.

Consequential Injury Or Expansion Of The Claim

As mentioned above, when the primary injury is shown to have arisen out of and in the course of employment, every natural consequence that flows from the injury similarly arises out of the employment unless it is the result of an independent intervening cause attributed to the claimant's own intentional conduct.

As also mentioned, if your doctor changes or expands your diagnosis, you may need to request to expand the claim. You must wait until the original claim is accepted before claiming a consequential injury or requesting expansion of the claim.

What Is A Schedule Award?

A "Schedule Award" is an award for any *permanent* impairment due to the *accepted* injury. **Injury to the spine (neck and back), brain and heart are specifically excluded by the statute.** However, *permanent impairment of the arms and legs due to a back or neck injury is included* and awards for those injuries are possible. In order to file a schedule award, you must:

1) Reach maximum medical improvement (MMI) of the accepted injury.

2) Request a medical exam according to the procedures outlined in the ***AMA Guides to the Evaluation of Permanent Impairment, fifth edition (AMA Guides).***

3) Request a medical report giving a specific % impairment due to the accepted injury using the AMA Guides and citing specific pages, charts and tables that were used when making the determination.

4) Submit a CA-7 with Section 2 box d checked off with the medical report attached.

The medical report must be clear enough for reasonably intelligent Claims Examiners to be able to follow the reasoning if they have a copy of the AMA Guides to refer to. Doctors must provide the numbers of the tables, figures, and procedures that they used to come to their opinions. Doctors must also provide the numbers of the pages where those tables, figures, and procedures can be found. A District Medical Advisor will review the medical evidence and offer an opinion. The Claims Examiner will make a decision based on the opinions provided. The amount of the award is based on the % permanent impairment, times the number of weeks of pay allowed for that part of the body, times the employee's weekly compensation rate.

You cannot receive a schedule award and continuing benefits for the same period for the same injury!!

If you apply for a schedule award while you are still receiving continuing benefits, the continuing benefits will be suspended until the schedule award is exhausted. The result is that you effectively lose your schedule award because you will receive it at the expense of your continuing benefits. There is no time limit on when you can apply for a schedule award. It is usually best to wait until you return to work or retire before you apply for a schedule award because the award is not affected by retirement benefits.

How Much Can I Get For Permanent Impairment?

The amount of compensation that you can receive for a permanent injury is based on a "schedule" which awards a *set* number of weeks of benefits for impairment to certain parts of the body. It is very cut and dried. **There is no negotiation or "settlement." *There is no additional compensation for pain and suffering or willful negligence of the employer.*** The Compensation Schedule tells you how much each body part is worth if it were 100% impaired. When your doctor does a Permanent Impairment Exam (PIE) according to the procedures in the *AMA Guide To The Evaluation Of Permanent Impairment, 5th edition*, the percentage of impairment is multiplied by the number of weeks on the schedule. (E.g., 10% impairment of the arm is worth 31.2 weeks of benefits.) There are maximum impairments for certain conditions. This is especially true in figuring impairment to the upper extremities (arms). Your doctor's calculation of your permanent impairment must include these maximums if they apply to your injury.

(E.g., maximum for impairment to the arm due to motor deficit because of damage to the ulnar nerve above the forearm is 46%. A 10% impairment would have to be multiplied by the 46% maximum = 4.6% X 312 weeks= 14.4 weeks of benefits.)

Failing to apply the maximum impairments is one of the most common mistakes that doctors make when writing a Permanent Impairment Evaluation. Whatever the compensation is, IT IS NEVER ENOUGH!!

Permanent Impairment Compensation Schedule

(Amounts are based on 100% impairment. Your % impairment will be multiplied by the number of weeks below)

Arm	312 weeks
Leg	288 weeks
Hand	244 weeks
Foot	205 weeks
Kidney	156 weeks
Larynx	160 weeks
Lung	156 weeks
Penis	205 weeks
Testicle	52 weeks
Tongue	160 weeks
Ovary (Including fallopian tubes)	52 weeks
Uterus/cervix	205
Vulva/vagina	205

Compensation for loss of binocular vision or for loss of 80 percent or more of the vision of an eye is the same as for the loss of the eye. The degree of loss of vision or hearing is determined without regard to correction; that is, improvements obtainable with the use of eyeglasses, contact lenses and hearing aids are not considered in establishing the percentage of impairment. *The law does not allow for payment of a scheduled award for impairment to the BACK (unless it causes impairment to the arms or legs), HEART or BRAIN.*

HOW LONG CAN I RECEIVE BENEFITS?

You can theoretically keep receiving federal workers compensation benefits indefinitely. However, there are at least five ways that your benefits can stop:

1.) Termination of monetary benefits due to a return to work. (Medical benefits should continue.)

2.) Termination of benefits because all residuals from the accepted injury have ceased and there is no longer any disability related to the accepted condition.

3.) Termination of benefits Under section 8106.

4.) Reduction in benefits due to your Wage Earning Capacity.

5.) Election of Disability Retirement Benefits from the Office Of Personal Management (OPM).

GOING BACK TO WORK

Restoration Rights

If you recover from your injury and are able to return to work within a short period of time, you will probably not have any trouble going back to work. However, if you have repeated injuries, or your injury is not expected to get any better, your Employer may not want to take you back. **If you have been out of work for an extended period of time, and it looks like you will be out for a year or more, your employer can separate you even if you are still collecting OWCP benefits.** However, you have restoration rights under the FECA. They are enforced through the Merit Systems Protection Board (MSPB). You do not have to be a veteran to have restoration rights enforced by the MSPB. If you feel that your restoration rights have been violated, you may file a complaint with the MSPB.

1.) If you completely recover from a work-related injury within a year, you are entitled to return to your old position even if you have been replaced.

2.) If you completely recover after more than a year, you have a right to the next available opening.

3.) If you partially recover, refusal to reinstate you must not be arbitrary or capricious.

If you completely recover from your injury and you are able to return to your regular job without restrictions, your benefits will probably be terminated because you will no longer be considered disabled due to your accepted work-related injury. If you have actually recovered, and you are able to return to your job, **you must protect your restoration rights by requesting reinstatement with the Employer within 30 days of the termination of OWCP benefits because you are no longer disabled due to your injury.** If you are denied reinstatement because of an injury that has *not* been accepted as work related, you are not entitled to restoration rights or compensation. However, you still have the right not to be discriminated against if you are a qualified individual with a disability. You may file a complaint with the EEOC if you feel that you are being denied reinstatement because of your disability.

ALL DISABILITY HAS CEASED AND/OR DISABILITY IS NO LONGER RELATED TO THE ACCEPTED INJURY

After an injury has been accepted as work-related, OWCP is not allowed to simply terminate compensation without establishing that the disability has ceased or that it was no longer related to your job. Anna M. Baline, 26 ECAB 351; Leon Altmann, 30 ECAB 674; Patricia Johnson, 34 ECAB 391 (1982). OWCP can only meet this burden by probative, well-rationalized medical evidence. That is, the same kind of medical evidence that you had to provide to get the claim accepted in the first place. Buddy R. Lundy, 95-2220 (10/7/96) citing in fn.11, George Randolph Taylor, 6 ECAB 986 (1954); Frederick L. Fields, 95-136 (4/10/96). The inadequacy or absence of a report in support of continuing benefits is not sufficient to support termination, and benefits should not be suspended for that reason. The Office has the burden of proof to justify the termination of benefits by positive and specific evidence that injury-related disability has ceased. Sometimes they do this by agreeing that you are disabled, but arguing that the disability is from an underlying condition that has not been accepted. This can leave you with no workers compensation benefits even though everyone agrees that you are unable to do your job. For example:

1) Your doctors agree that you are still totally disabled due to a herniated disc. However, your accepted condition was a lumbar strain over a year ago. OWCP terminates benefits because your doctors agree that the strain has resolved and disability is no longer related to the accepted lumbar strain.

2) You have a torn rotator cuff. Your doctors agree that your neck problem has resolved but that you are totally disabled until your shoulder surgery is authorized. Your claim was accepted as a cervical strain. Authorization for surgery is denied and your benefits are terminated because your disability is no longer related to the resolved cervical strain.

3) Your doctors agree that you have a severe underlying back condition which is aggravated by your work. The claim was accepted as a temporary aggravation of the underlying condition. Your doctors agree that your condition is repeatedly aggravated by your job. OWCP treats each aggravation as a separate claim. They argue that all disability ceases after you stop working for a while so, until you go back to work, all disability has ceased. (The best way to fight this is to show that the aggravations caused cumulative, permanent damage.)

This is why it is so important to make sure that the claim is properly accepted and expanded to cover all of your work-related injuries.

REFUSAL OF A SUITABLE JOB OFFER

Under section 8106(c)(2) of the FECA, the Office may terminate the monetary compensation of an employee who "refuses or neglects to work after suitable work is offered to, procured by, or secured for him." <u>Herman L. Anderson</u>, 36 ECAB 253 (1984) This section is meant to punish a worker for refusing to return to work.

Sometimes the employer will offer you a limited duty position that is within your medical restrictions. When the injury is temporary, this can work out quite well. However, when the injury is permanent, the job that is offered is often far less desirable than the one you had when you were injured. In addition, there is usually no opportunity for advancement in a rehab job and union seniority does not apply for a more desirable shift or days off. If you are forced to accept a limited duty position that you really don't want, keep in mind that you still have the right to apply for any position that you could apply for before you were injured, as long as you can perform the "core duties" of the job.[4]

If the Department of Labor finds that the Employer's job offer is suitable, the department informs the injured worker that they have 30 days

---

4   If you can perform the "core duties" of the job, are otherwise qualified for the position, and are refused the job because of your disability, or perceived disability, you may have an EEO complaint but you should contact a counselor within 30 days.

to show that the job is not suitable. This is so the claimant's attending physician will have an opportunity to determine whether the claimant can perform the job. Under the "Maggie Moore Doctrine"[5] if the OWCP Claims Examiner does not find that you have proven that the limited duty job is not suitable after the thirty days, you have an additional 15 days to accept the job, or they will terminate your benefits under section 8106. **This will also terminate your right to receive a permanent impairment award for that injury.**

You are still entitled to receive medical benefits even after your monetary benefits have been terminated under section 8106. If your doctor says you can do the job, you will probably need to at least try it. If your doctor says that you can't do the job, OWCP may send you for a second opinion. If that doctor disagrees with your doctor, you may be sent to a medical referee to resolve the conflict in medical opinion. If the medical referee agrees that you can do the job, and the report is valid, you will probably have to try the job or risk losing your monetary benefits permanently. **Fear of future injury is not considered a valid reason to refuse a position.** If you are injured again, you may file a new claim for aggravation of your pre-existing condition by job duties. However, in some cases you may have to decide to risk termination of benefits rather than to risk further injury.

---

5   Maggie L. Moore, Docket No. 90- 1291, issued March 8, 1991).

Requirements of a Suitable Job Offer

An offer of limited duty work which the employer simply says complies with an attending physician's medical restrictions is not sufficient for OWCP to meet its burden under section 8106(c)(2). The job duties and physical requirements of the job need to be fully described, and a physician must review the physical requirements to determine whether they are in the employee's physical capability. Employers must provide a job offer that injured workers can take to their doctors for an opinion on whether they can perform the job. The Office's procedures provide that, to be valid, an offer of limited duty **must be in writing** and it must include:

1) **a description of the duties to be performed**
2) **the specific physical requirements of the position and any special demands of the work-load or unusual working conditions**
3) **the organizational and geographical location of the job**
4) **hours and days off**
5) **rate of pay**
6) **the date on which the job will first be available; and the date by which a response to the job offer is required**

The burden is on the employer and OWCP to produce rationalized medical evidence that you are medically able to do the job. Where a conflict of medical evidence exists as to whether you can perform a limited duty position the Office has not met its burden to justify termination of benefits. Buddy R. Lundy, supra; Dineen Jordan, 95-994 (9/18/95);

Isaac Smith, 94-148 (5/9/95); Eric J. Heckmann, 93-1985 (9/6/94); see also, 5 USC §8123(a). This is why the Office may continue to send you to second opinions and medical referees at least once a year if your doctors continue to say that you cannot work.

Second Opinions (Secops) and Medical Referees

OWCP can send you for a second opinion (Secop) or to a Medical Referee whenever they think it is necessary. It is not always a bad thing. Some of these doctors are very bad no matter what you do, but some are quite good and feel strongly that they are obligated to be objective. You MUST be cooperative and compliant with medical exams ordered by the Department of Labor. I advise my clients to do the following:

1) Notice if the exam is being ordered and paid for by the Department of Labor or your Agency. A fitness for duty exam ordered by the employer may be useful for them to determine work capacity, but it cannot be used to resolve a conflict in the medical evidence regarding your entitlement to benefits because it is not impartial. If you do not submit to the exam, you may be disciplined by your employer, but it should not affect your claim.

2) Gather any medical evidence that you want the doctors to see in case they are not given the entire record. Do not assume that they have all of your medical records or that they will take the time to look at them even if they do have the entire file. However, you can't force them to look at it. Referees are usually more open to other opinions than the second opinion doctors.

3) Write down relevant dates, treatments, and other relevant information so you can remember them to tell the doctor.

4) Be cooperative and polite no matter how obnoxious or negligent the doctor seems. If the doctor stops the exam because you are rude or belligerent, OWCP can suspend your benefits for months while they schedule another appointment, if they schedule another appointment at all. You will have no way to get your benefits reinstated while you wait…and wait. You will not get those benefits back either.

5) Remember, if the doctor's report is not in your favor, it is easier to refute when you are cooperative and the doctor is an arrogant jerk that makes mistakes.

6) Do not exaggerate or diminish your symptoms. They have tests that they do to test the validity of your responses. Invalid results are worse than none at all. Be honest, straightforward, and specific. Use the dates that you wrote down. The doctor does not understand your job. Explain it carefully. Inconsistency is bad. Sincerity is good.

BEWARE! **SOME AGENCIES ENGAGE IN SURVEILLANCE AND THEY WILL SHOW THE VIDEO TO THE DOCTOR AND ASK QUESTIONS ABOUT IT!**

Vocational Rehabilitation and Wage Earning Capacity

5 USC § 8115 of the Federal Employees' Compensation Act pertains to the determination of Wage Earning Capacity (WEC) and Section 8104(a) vocational rehabilitation. In recent years, the federal agencies, especially the Postal Service, have been unwilling, or unable, to provide "Rehab" positions to the extent that they had previously. It is becoming more and more common for an employing Agency to simply refuse to provide a rehab position, preferring to pay the OWCP benefits until OWCP can determine the employee's Wage Earning Capacity, based on a private sector job description, and reduce or terminate their benefits based on that determination. This involves two very popular misconceptions.

1) **YES, the employer CAN separate you if the employer cannot reasonably accommodate your restrictions even though you were injured at work.**

2) **NO, It is NOT necessary for OWCP to actually find you a job in order to reduce your benefits based on your theoretical wage earning capacity (WEC)!**

Generally, I tell my clients that it is a very good idea to begin thinking about what you may want to do for a job if your employing agency refuses to take you back. **If you go into the initial meeting with the Vocational Rehab Counselor with some idea of what you want to do, and a plan that you would like to try to implement, you will have more**

control over the process! If you resist the idea of doing anything, and go into it with no idea of what you want to do, you will be pushed through the process anyway and you will probably not be happy with the result. If you fail to cooperate at all, your benefits will probably be suspended for non-cooperation. If this happens, it is very difficult to turn around. This is the procedure that the Rehab Counselor usually follows:

1) They ask the Employing Agency if they can provide a limited duty position.

2) If not, they interview injured workers to determine what education, work experience, and training they already have. At this point, it is a very good idea to go into the interview with some kind of idea of what you may want to do.

3) They review the injured worker's medical restrictions. (Past, present and subsequent restrictions from work-related and not work-related injuries)

4) They look in the Dictionary of Occupational Titles (DOT) to find a job that fits the injured worker's education and previous work experience and is within the injured worker's medical restrictions.

5) They determine if the job is "reasonably available" within the injured worker's commuting area and the average wage for that job in that area.

6) If the Rehab Counselor is convinced that additional training will result in a substantially higher WEC, the Rehab counselor may recommend additional training including up to two years of school. This is relatively rare.

7) If the Rehab Counselor recommends additional training, and the Claims Examiner can be convinced to send you to school, you may get paid to get a degree or certificate.

8) If the Rehab Counselor identifies a job that is within your education, experience, training and medical restrictions, your WEC will be based on that job.

9) Your benefits will be reduced by your WEC.

If your WEC is less than you were making when you were injured, you will still be paid for your lowered wage earning capacity (LWEC). This is determined by applying the "Shadrick" formula. The suitability of the position and the computation of the compensation rate are complicated. If you have additional questions, you can ask your Claims Examiner in Boston or consult with a federal workers compensation attorney.

If you do any work outside of your federal agency after you are injured, including work for no pay, your WEC may be based on that work if it "fairly and reasonably" represents your wage earning capacity. The criteria for whether the work can be used as a basis for your WEC are very complicated and inconsistently applied. If you have questions, you should ask the Claims Examiner to explain it or consult with a federal workers compensation attorney.

What If I Apply For Disability Retirement?

DO NOT RESIGN!! If you get a letter giving you the choice to return to work, resign, or apply for disability retirement, it is better to let them separate you because they can't accommodate you than it is to simply resign. *If you quit, all OWCP benefits could stop!* If you resign, you may still be able to apply for Disability Retirement within a year if you can prove that your resignation was related to your disability, but it is *much* more difficult.

You may apply, and qualify, for Disability Retirement benefits (OPM) and OWCP benefits at the same time, however you can only *receive* one of them at a time. You must elect one or the other. The election is revocable so you can stay on Disability Retirement until your claim is accepted and then elect OWCP benefits until you are no longer disabled from the work-related injury. OWCP benefits are usually, but not always, better than Disability Retirement benefits. However, if you are collecting OPM benefits, you can work at another job and make up to 80% of your past wage without it affecting your benefits. You can also receive a schedule award while receiving disability retirement benefits. Wages are subtracted from OWCP benefits dollar for dollar. **If you ever want to receive Disability Retirement benefits, you *must apply* for benefits within *one year* of separation from federal service whether or not you elect to receive them right away.**

SAMPLES OF THE MOST COMMON CLAIMS

Preparing A Repetitive Motion Claim

When preparing a claim for a repetitive motion injury you should:

1) **Get an accurate and complete medical diagnosis of your condition.**

2) Make a **list of all of your job duties** and how long you spend at each one and, when applicable, how many repetitions per minute you perform.

3) **Show the list to your doctor** and describe and/or demonstrate each job duty.

4) Request a **rationalized medical opinion** citing which specific job duties caused or aggravated your diagnosed condition and how they did it.

5) **File a CA2** with the above **medical report** and a *consistent* employee statement.

Chapter 3-0600 section 8c in the FECA Manual defines objective medical evidence to determine if a claimant has Carpal Tunnel Syndrome:

> c. Carpal Tunnel Syndrome. This condition involves the compression of the medial nerve between the longitudinal tendons of the wrist musculature and the transverse superficial carpal ligament along the palmer aspect of the wrist (see Exhibit 9). Symptoms resulting from this compression include pain, numbness, tingling, and weakness of the affected hand (usually the dominant one, though bilateral involvement does occur). Causes which may be work-related include constant exertion and/or repetitive motion with the wrist flexed or extended against resistance, and acute trauma. The medical report should contain clear evidence that the disease is present.

Among the clinical findings are the following:

1) Phalen's Sign. This test is positive if maintenance of forced hyperflexion for one minute precipitates pain and paresthesia.

2) Tinel's Sign. This test is positive if tapping over the medial nerve at the wrist produces pain.

3) Neurological Abnormalities. These include decreased sensation over the palmar aspect of the end joints of the same three and one half digits and atrophy of the thenar eminence in severe cases.

4) Decreased nerve conduction velocity (NCV) as measured during nerve conduction test. The test results should include an evaluation as to whether the velocities obtained are normal or not.

5) Decreased muscle motor activity as measured by electromyography (EMG). The test results should clearly indicate whether the results are within normal limits or are abnormal. An opinion as to the cause of the abnormality may also be present.

Make sure your doctor understands exactly what you do and can list your specific job duties in a report on causation. Other repetitive motion injuries to the forearm, elbow or shoulder should be separately diagnosed and addressed. Cervical (neck) conditions also sometimes result in arm pain and numbness. It is important that the diagnosis is complete and accurate. *If a less serious condition is accepted, medical expenses, residual disability, or permanent impairment from a more serious condition will not be covered unless the claim is expanded to include that specific condition. An MRI as well as above tests may be useful in diagnosing* these other conditions. Consistency is important! **Do not change your description of your duties without explanation!**

"Stress" Claims

Stress claims are extremely difficult but not impossible under the right circumstances. In order to be compensated for a work-related emotional injury, **it is not sufficient to simply show that work-related stress caused or aggravated the emotional condition.** You cannot get compensation for disability caused by most work-related stress. **The injury must be caused or aggravated by** *specific compensable factors of employment.* **Most factors of employment that cause stress are not compensable.** The compensable factors of employment do not have to be the sole cause of the injury, but the claimant must provide medical evidence that shows that *those specific factors* caused, aggravated, or significantly contributed to, the current disability. A long list of non-compensable employment factors (such as examples of immoral, unjust conduct of coworkers or incompetent management decisions) will only serve to undermine your argument that the compensable factors caused, or significantly contributed to, your condition.

Compensable Factors of Employment

The Board has held that the following may be considered compensable factors of employment:

- Emotional reactions to situations in which an employee is trying to meet his or her position requirements may be compensable (e.g., Claims Examiner who files a claim alleging that his emotional condition was caused by the pressures of trying to meet the production standards of his job).

- Stress from supervisory duties, such as directing subordinates to complete projects, attempting to meet deadlines with limited staff, working overtime hours.

- Unusually heavy workload and imposition of unreasonable deadlines. (You must provide *objective* evidence of workload and/or unreasonableness of deadline.)

- Depression or anxiety as a result of physical restrictions from an *accepted* physical injury.

- Repeated, unprovoked verbal altercations regarding job duties in front of coworkers. (Personal arguments or arguments where both parties are at fault are usually not compensable.)

- Physical altercations. Usually physical altercations with coworkers or supervisors are compensable unless the injured worker initiated the incident or participated other than to defend themselves.

- *Some* confrontations while performing duties as a representative of a labor union.

Noncompensable Factors of Employment

The following are usually *not* considered compensable factors of employment:

- Anxiety about job security.

- Frustration from not being permitted to work in a particular environment or particular position.

- Reaction to an administrative action such as discipline, transfer, general announcement, that is not done in error. (Error *must* be corroborated by a grievance or EEO complaint *decided*, not settled, in your favor.)

- Frustration from witnessing incompetent management that does not *directly* affect your ability to do *your* job.

- Frustration from witnessing incompetent, immoral or irresponsible behavior of coworkers that does not directly affect your ability to do your job.

- Harassment or discrimination that is not corroborated by a finding of discrimination by the EEOC, grievance procedure, or, in some cases, *very* strong statements by coworkers.

- Any confrontations, physical or verbal, that are caused by personal relationships outside of work and do not specifically involve work duties.

Harassment And Discrimination

About half of the injured workers that come to our office believe that they have a claim for emotional injury due to harassment or "discrimination." Unfortunately, most harassment is not considered a compensable factor of employment. It is usually best to try to avoid framing the issue as a claim for disability due to harassment. Discrimination usually has to be corroborated by a finding of fact in another forum. The most often cited case in emotional claims is <u>Lillian Cutler</u>, 28 ECAB 125 (1976). This case explains some of the basic criteria for harassment to be considered a compensable factor of employment. The requirements are vague. It is usually easier to say what is not a compensable factor of employment in a harassment claim than it is to say what is. The process is very subjective. There is no magic formula.

Each case needs to be individually developed to present *convincing* **evidence that the incidents of harassment actually took place, that they were related to the job, and that they caused or aggravated an emotional condition.** The credibility of the claimant is *extremely* important in these cases. **Witnesses must be able to testify about seeing** *you* **harassed. Testimony about being harassed themselves will be ignored as irrelevant.**

Each incident of harassment that is cited as a compensable factor of employment will be analyzed according to the following criteria:

1) **Whether the alleged harassment or discrimination did in fact happen.** When an employee files a claim for disability due to work-related stress due to harassment or discrimination, the employee

must show that the incidents of harassment or discrimination actually took place. <u>Karen E. Humphrey</u>, 44 ECAB 908 (1993) "Mere perceptions" of harassment are not compensable. <u>Ruth C. Borden</u> 43 ECAB 146 (1991) Events must be corroborated by a finding of fact by another agency such as the EEOC, MSPB, the grievance procedure (<u>Gregory Meisenburg</u>, 44 ECAB 527 (1993)) or, in some instances by "reliable, probative and substantial" corroboration by a coworker or supervisor.

2) Whether the "harassment" was reasonably justified **<u>Barbara J. Nicholson</u> 45 ECAB 803 (1993).**

3) Whether the harassment or discrimination was related to job duties. **Personal harassment that does not affect the employee's ability to perform the job is usually not compensable. The harassment must be related to the job.**

4) Whether the harassment or discrimination caused or aggravated the diagnosed emotional condition. **As in any claim for compensation, there must be evidence of causation.**

It is very rare to win a claim for emotional injury due to harassment at work. It is extremely subjective, and cooperative witnesses are very hard to find. It is usually better to try to find another compensable factor of employment.

Administrative Actions

Administrative actions are very rarely found to be factors of employment. If the employee is alleging administrative actions as harassment, they must show that the actions were not only unfair, but that they were erroneous or that the administrative process is being abused to harass the claimant. Error and abuse usually have to be corroborated by an actual finding of fact by *another agency* or forum such as the EEOC, MSPB, a grievance or an arbitration decision that finds that the Agency has erred. *A settlement without a finding of any wrongdoing is not sufficient to show error.* **If there is no finding of error from another fact-finding process, it is unlikely that the OWCP will make a finding of fact regarding error in an administrative action.** Since only a decision that there was error on the part of the employer will be considered proof of error in an administrative decision, **claimants and their Representatives should consider the effect of a settlement or resolution of a grievance or EEO complaint on a potential OWCP claim.** Repeated discipline and withdrawal of discipline may be an example of abuse of the administrative process for the purpose of harassment in some cases. However, the mere withdrawal of discipline does not necessarily mean that there was error. OWCP must find the administrative action unreasonable. Each case is very fact specific. It is amazing what they find reasonable.

How Do I Prepare A Claim For Compensation for Work-Related Stress?

1) Make a list of what you believe to be the compensable factors of employment including dates and specific circumstances surrounding each incident. (You can usually only go back three years.)

2) Share these incidents with your psychologist or psychiatrist and ask if they believe that any of those *specific* incidents caused, aggravated, or contributed to, your condition. It is important that these incidents go into the doctor's medical notes as soon as possible. Your doctor must give a clear medical diagnosis, demonstrate knowledge of the circumstances and history of the condition and any testing or treatment you have received, and provide a clear, rationalized opinion citing the *specific* compensable factors of employment, that caused, aggravated, or contributed to your diagnosed condition, including dates and circumstances.

3) File a CA2 if the incidents cover more than one shift or a CA1 if a specific incident caused, aggravated, or contributed to your condition.

DEATH BENEFITS

Death as a result of an accepted work-related injury is relatively rare. However, under certain circumstances, OWCP is obligated to pay benefits to survivors of a federal employee who dies as a result of an accepted work-related injury. The FECA provides for compensation at 5 USC 8133:

1) To the widow or widower, if there is no child, 50 percent.

2) To the widow or widower, if there is a child, 45 percent and in addition 15 percent for each child not to exceed a total of 75 percent for the widow or widower and children.

3) To the children, if there is no widow or widower, 40 percent for one child and 15 percent additional for each additional child not to exceed a total of 75 percent, divided among the children share and share alike.

4) To the parents, if there is no widow, widower, or child, as follows -

   (A) 25 percent if one parent was wholly dependent on the employee at the time of death and the other was not dependent to any extent;

   (B) 20 percent to each if both were wholly dependent; or

   (C) a proportionate amount in the discretion of the Secretary of Labor if one or both were partly dependent. If there is a widow, widower, or child, so much of the percentages are payable as, when added to the total percentages payable to the widow, widower, and children, will not exceed a total of 75 percent.

5) To the brothers, sisters, grandparents, and grandchildren, if there is no widow, widower, child, or dependent parent, as follows -

(A) 20 percent if one was wholly dependent on the employee at the time of death;

(B) 30 percent if more than one was wholly dependent divided among the dependents share and share alike; or

(C) 10 percent if no one is wholly dependent but one or more is partly dependent, divided among the dependents share and share alike.

There are some additional rules and hoops to jump through in order to receive these benefits. If you have questions, you may call your Claims Examiner or consult a federal workers compensation attorney.

Why Do I Have Trouble Finding an Attorney to Represent Me?

If you are a federal employee, and you have been injured, you have probably had trouble finding an attorney who is willing, and able, to help you. It is a complicated, sometimes arbitrary, bureaucratic system with no judicial review. There is no fee shifting. Claimants have to pay their own attorney's fees, win or lose. The employer and OWCP never pay attorney's fees in a federal workers compensation claim. OWCP does not pay your attorney's fees even if it is their mistake or negligence that caused the need for an attorney.

It is illegal for an attorney to represent you for a percentage of your award if you win. Although the attorney may take a refundable retainer to cover expenses, it must be kept in a client escrow account until the bill is approved. The statute requires the attorney to present the injured worker with a "proposed bill" that is itemized and includes a "reasonable hourly rate" along with a client fee opinion form. If the client/injured worker signs the form agreeing that the proposed fee is correct and reasonable, the fee is "deemed approved." If the client/injured worker disagrees with the proposed fee, the attorney must ask OWCP (the same Claims Examiner that just approved the claim) to approve the fee. This can take a very long time. It can take years to get a $300 fee approved before the attorney can take the money from the client trust account and/or send a bill.

The whole process is so complicated, unpredictable and time consuming that most attorneys just don't want to deal with it. The lack of judicial review means that if the Employees' Compensation Appeals Board (ECAB) makes a decision, there is nowhere else for you to go. They interpret the statute and make the rules. You do not get your "day in court." The District Office, the Branch of Hearings and Review and the ECAB are all parts of the Department of Labor (DOL), which makes the decisions and then reviews them.

There are no consequences to OWCP if it makes mistakes or if there is a delay in payment or treatment. But injured workers may suffer permanent physical damage while they wait for treatment, or lose their houses to foreclosure while they wait for the mistakes to be corrected. The OWCP is not accountable to anyone other than, theoretically, Congress. However, even Congress does not appear to know how to fix this system so that it is fair and equitable. They will make an "Inquiry," but they are usually answered in a form letter saying that the claim is "being adjudicated" and that is as far as most of them will go. There are no real consequences to any of the parties involved except the injured worker/client. The attorney is forced to ask for an hourly rate from their clients only, win or lose. If clients are unhappy with the result, they can contest the fee and the attorney will not get paid for a very long time, if at all. That is why you have trouble finding an attorney who can help you.

OWCP Hierarchy In Massachusetts

Secretary of Labor: Elaine L. Chao
U.S. Department of Labor
 200 Constitution Ave.
NW, Washington, DC 20210
202-693-6000

Employees' Compensation Appeals Board
200 Constitution Ave. NW, Room N-2609
Washington, DC 20210
202-693-5037

Director of OWCP: Shelby Hallmark
202-693-0031

Branch of Hearings and Review
Office of Workers' Compensation Programs
P.O. Box 37117
Washington, DC 20013-7117
202-693-0045

Regional Director for Northeast Region (consists of the New York and Boston offices): Jaye Weisman
201 Varick Street
Room 750, New York, NY 10014
646-264-3100

Claims Examiner
Boston District Office
U.S. Department of Labor, OWCP, DFEC
JFK Federal Building, Room E-260
Boston, MA 02203
617-624-6600
Mailing Address
U.S. Dept. Of Labor, OWCP, DFEC
Office Of Workers' Compensation Programs
P. O. Box 8300 - Region 1 BOSTON, London, Kentucky 40742-830

Employer Point Person (Injury Compensation Specialist or designated person in Human Resources)

Claimant- You!

INDEX TO SECTION ON MASSACHUSETTS SYSTEM

INDEX TO SECTION ON FEDERAL WORKERS COMPENSATION